The Labyrinth of the World and the Paradise of the Heart

THE LABYRINTH OF THE WORLD

THE
LABYRINTH OF THE WORLD

AND THE

PARADISE OF THE HEART

BY

(JOHN) AMOS (KOMENSKY)

Johann *Comenius*

(COMENIUS)

EDITED AND TRANSLATED BY

COUNT LÜTZOW

Member of the Bohemian Society of Sciences, and of the Bohemian Academy ;
formerly Deputy for Bohemia in the Austrian Parliament ; Author of
" A History of Bohemian Literature," " Bohemia : an Historical
Sketch," " Prague" (Mediæval Towns Series)

LONDON

SWAN SONNENSCHEIN & CO., Lim.

PATERNOSTER SQUARE, E.C.

1901

"Nevzali jsme ssebou
Nic, po vsem veta
Jen bibli Kralickou
Labyrint sveta."

"Nothing have we taken with us,
Everything is lost ;
We have but our bible of Kralice,
Our ' Labyrinth of the World.' "

—Song of the Bohemian Exiles.

Printed by Cowan & Co., Ltd., Perth.

CONTENTS

		Page
INTRODUCTION -	- - - - -	11
DEDICATION -	- - - - -	53
TO THE READER -	- - - - -	55

CHAPTER I.
On the Causes of this my Pilgrimage through the World - - - - - - 59

CHAPTER II.
The Pilgrim obtains Impudence as a Guide - - 61

CHAPTER III.
Falsehood joins Them - - - 64

CHAPTER IV.
The Pilgrim receives a Bridle and Spectacles - 66

CHAPTER V.
The Pilgrim views the World from on High - - 69

CHAPTER VI.
Fate distributes Vocations - - - - 74

CHAPTER VII.
The Pilgrim beholds the Market-place of the World 77

CHAPTER VIII.
The Pilgrim beholds the State of Matrimony - 89

CHAPTER IX.
The Pilgrim examines the Order of the Tradesmen - 99

6 CONTENTS

Page

CHAPTER X.
The Pilgrim beholds the Fate of the Men of Learning, at first generally - - - - 114

CHAPTER XI.
The Pilgrim comes among the Philosophers publicly 129

CHAPTER XII.
The Pilgrim studies Alchemy - - - 146

CHAPTER XIII.
The Pilgrim beholds the Rosicrucians - - 150

CHAPTER XIV.
The Pilgrim studies Medicine - - - 157

CHAPTER XV.
The Pilgrim beholds Jurisprudence - - - 160

CHAPTER XVI.
The Pilgrim witnesses the Promotion of Masters and
Doctors - - - - - - 163

CHAPTER XVII.
The Pilgrim beholds the Estate of Priesthood - 166

CHAPTER XVIII.
The Pilgrim beholds the Christian Religion - - 171

CHAPTER XIX.
The Pilgrim beholds the Order of the Magistrates - 187

CHAPTER XX.
The Estate of Soldiery - - - - 198

CHAPTER XXI.
The Estate of the Knights - - - 204

Page

CHAPTER XXII.

The Pilgrim finds Himself among the Newsmen - 209

CHAPTER XXIII.

The Pilgrim beholds the Castle of Fortune, and firstly, the Entrance to It - - - - 212

CHAPTER XXIV.

The Pilgrim beholds the Ways of the Wealthy . - 216

CHAPTER XXV.

The Ways of the Voluptuous in the World - - 220

CHAPTER XXVI.

The Ways of the Great of the World - - - 226

CHAPTER XXVII.

Fama ferme vulgi opinione constat - - - 229

CHAPTER XXVIII.

The Pilgrim begins to despair and to quarrel with his Guides - - - - - 235

CHAPTER XXIX.

The Pilgrim beholds the Palace of Wisdom, the Queen of the World - - - - 239

CHAPTER XXX.

How the Pilgrim was impeached in the Palace of Wisdom - - - - - - 241

CHAPTER XXXI.

Solomon, with a Large Multitude, comes to the Palace of Wisdom - - - - - 247

8   CONTENTS

                                                        Page
                     .   CHAPTER XXXII.
The Pilgrim beholds the Secret Judgments and the
    Government of the World   -   -   -   250

                  CHAPTER XXXIII.
Solomon discloses the Vanities and Deceits of the
    World   -   -   -   -   -   -   265

                  CHAPTER XXXIV.
Solomon is deceived and misled   -   -   -   268

                  CHAPTER XXXV.
Solomon's Company is dispersed and captured, and
    perishes by Terrible Fashions of Death -   -   271

                  CHAPTER XXXVI.
The Pilgrim desires to flee from the World -   -   274

                  CHAPTER XXXVII.
The Pilgrim finds his Way Home   -   -   -   277

                  CHAPTER XXXVIII.
The Pilgrim receives Christ as his Guest   -   -   280

                  CHAPTER XXXIX.
Their Betrothal   -   -   -   -   -   283

                  CHAPTER XL.
The Pilgrim is as one transformed   -   -   -   293

                  CHAPTER XLI.
The Pilgrim is ordered to enter the Invisible Church   295

                  CHAPTER XLII.
The Light of the Inward Christians -   -   -   300

Page

CHAPTER XLIII.

The Liberty of those Hearts that are devoted to God   305

CHAPTER XLIV.

The Regulations of the Inward Christian   -   -   308

CHAPTER XLV.

Everything is light and easy to the Hearts that are
devoted to God   -   -   -   -   -   315

CHAPTER XLVI.

The Holy Ones have Abundance of Everything   -   318

CHAPTER XLVII.

The Safety of those who are devoted to God   -   321

CHAPTER XLVIII.

The Godly have Peace on all Sides   -   -   -   325

CHAPTER XLIX.

The Godly have Constant Delight within their Hearts   332

CHAPTER L.

The Pilgrim beholds the Christians according to their
States   -   -   -   -   -   -   334

CHAPTER LI.

The Death of Faithful Christians   -   -   -   339

CHAPTER LII.

The Pilgrim beholds the Glory of God   -   -   341

CHAPTER LIII.

The Pilgrim is received into God's Household   -   343

CHAPTER LIV.

The End of All   -   -   -   -   -   345

INTRODUCTION

I FEEL certain that it is venturesome to attempt to bring a work of a Bohemian writer before the English-speaking public, now the largest public of readers in the world. Even the name of my country has been known to English readers only in connection with associations that are both incongruous and absurd.

It seems to me certain that the judgment that Bohemian critics have passed on Komensky's masterpiece, the " Labyrinth of the World," claiming it to be one of the world's great books, is not unfounded or based on patriotic predilections. That the book is so little known must be attributed to various causes. Almost at the time that the " Labyrinth " appeared, Komensky's Church, the " Unity," as it was called, of the Bohemian or " Moravian " brethren, was expelled from Bohemia, and it became impossible for a book, written by so eminent a member of that community, to find readers in those countries where the language in which it was written was almost exclusively known. That language itself declined completely after Bohemian independence had perished in 1620, at the battle of the White Mountain, near Prague. These obstacles continued for many years. Dr.

von Criegern[1] tells us that in 1749 a list of "dangerous and forbidden books," published at Königgrätz, included the "Labyrinth." Even early in the nineteenth century an edition of the book was suppressed. I shall refer to these facts again later when mentioning the various editions of the "Labyrinth" and dealing with Komensky's religious views; yet it may be mentioned here already that the "Labyrinth" is singularly free from "odium theologicum." The Bohemians have always been devoted to the "Labyrinth." Its mysticism was very congenial to them, and the variety of picturesque incident that it contains appealed to an imaginative people. The book being prohibited, the few copies that escaped destruction passed from hand to hand secretly, and were safely hidden in the scattered cottages of the Bohemian peasants. The many Bohemian exiles who left their beloved country rather than forsake their creed often took the "Labyrinth" with them. With the "Bible of Kralice,"[2] it was almost their only worldly possession, according to the words of their song, quoted by me on the title-page of this book.

Komensky—or Comenius, as he has generally been called in England—never shared the fate of many Bohemian writers; that is to say, complete

---

[1] "Johann Amos Comenius als Theolog."

[2] This refers to a translation of the Bible that was the joint-work of several divines of the "Unity," assembled at Kralice, in Moravia, about the end of the sixteenth century. It is a model of Bohemian diction, and Komensky modelled his style on it, to a great extent, when writing the "Labyrinth."

oblivion. He has been saved from it by the fact
that some of his educational works, written in Latin,
have always been known to teachers. Thus his
" Janua Linguarum " was in use as a school-book
for nearly two centuries. An Anglo-Latin version
of it was published at Oxford as late as in 1800.
Some of Komensky's other educational works, such
as the " Orbispictus," also became widely known.
On the other hand, his later philosophical, or, as
he called them, " pansophic " works have obtained
but limited recognition. The power of condensing
his thoughts and concentrating his mind that
Komensky possessed when he wrote the " Labyrinth " failed him later in life, though the pansophic
works for a short time attracted some attention,
particularly in England.

To those who are not either professed pedagogues
or students for whom long-past theories on
natural history and natural philosophy—such as
we find in the pansophic works—have an historical
interest, Komensky's most valuable work will
always be the " Labyrinth of the World." It is a
work of the author's youth, though by no means
his first work ; and he who later in his life became
somewhat diffuse has here concentrated his ideas,
and given in a few pages an almost perfect picture
of the life and thought of Bohemia and Germany
as they appeared to one living in the early years
of the seventeenth century.

The " Labyrinth of the World and the Paradise
of the Heart "—to give the book its full name—
belongs to that large class of writings that are

founded on the world-old conceit that imagines
the world as a city and man as a pilgrim, who
beholds it and examines it. It is natural that this
allegorical idea took very different shapes in the
hands of different writers. Sometimes, as with
Komensky, the world appears twofold—the evil,
earthly world that is but mockery, and the "paradise of the heart" in which the soul finds solace,
even before its union with God, "the centre of all."
Oftener the latter ideal world only is delineated, as
in countless works, from Plato downward. It is, I
think, improbable that Komensky knew Plato's
writings, but I feel certain that he knew the quaint
work of the so-called Kebes,[1] entitled Πιναξ. There
is no doubt that this now little known work influenced Komensky to some extent. I have now
before me a copy of the edition of the book published at Leyden in 1640. It contains an engraving
that could almost be imagined as being an illustra-
tion of Komensky's allegorical work. We see the
gate of life, through which all must enter ; the
various streets in which men reside, according to
their callings ; and in the heights the dwellings of
eternal bliss. More's "Utopia" and Campanella's
"Civitas Solis" undoubtedly influenced Komensky
when writing the "Labyrinth," and he mentions
both More and Campanella by name in the book.
On the other hand, there is no trace in it of the

[1] This book was long attributed to Kebes, a disciple of
Plato. Recent research has rendered it probable that it
was written by a philosopher during the reign of the
Emperor Marcus Aurelius.

influence of "Verulamius," as Komensky always calls Bacon, though his later writings have evidence of a considerable study of the works of Bacon, whom he frequently mentions.[1] It may perhaps be conjectured that he only studied these works later, perhaps at Lissa.

The books, however, that influenced Komensky most when writing the "Labyrinth" were some of the works of John Valentine Andrea.[2] It is certain that Komensky studied the works of the Würtemberg divine during his stay at Brandeis; and it is obvious that some of these works, such as the "Fama Fraternitatis," "Roseæ Crucis," "Peregrini in Patria errores," "Civis Christianus," "Republicæ Christianopolitanæ Descriptio"—itself obviously an adaptation of Campanella's "Civitas Solis"—and others too numerous to mention, greatly influenced Komensky when writing the "Labyrinth." The passages culled from these and other works of Andrea that resemble passages in the "Labyrinth" have been very carefully collected by Dr. von Criegern in his "Comenius als Theolog." This valuable book is, unfortunately, tainted with the Teutonic mania that strives to deny all originality of thought to the Slavic race. The mere fact that these analogies are chosen from various different

[1] In his "Physica," Komensky writes that Verulamius and Campanella are "the two Hercules that have vanquished the monster Aristotle."

[2] A Lutheran divine, born 1586, and a very copious writer in the then fashionable allegorical manner. He was Court Chaplain at Stuttgart for many years, and then (Protestant) Abbot at Babenhausen, and afterwards at Adelsberg. He died at Stuttgart in 1654.

works of Andrea weakens Dr. von Criegern's argument. It is not my purpose to enter into this matter here. It is certain that the first chapter of the "Labyrinth" is little but a paraphrase of the opening part of Andrea's "Peregrinus," that the pilgrim's visit to the philosophers (chap. xi.) is largely founded on a passage of Andrea's "Mythologia Christiana," and that his visit to the Rosicrucians[1] is mainly copied from Andrea's writings concerning that community.[2] Yet this but slightly detracts from Komensky's originality of thought. It has already been noted that the conceit of a pilgrim travelling through the world, as well as the conception of an ideal city, are world-old ideas which belonged to Komensky, as rightly as to Andrea, whose "Republicæ Christianopoli Fanæ" is, as I have already noted, an adaptation of the "Civitas Solis." Even at a slight glance at Andrea's ponderous writings, it will be seen how Komensky has enriched and vivified those conceptions that he borrowed from him. Dr. von Criegern goes so far as to declare that even the pessimism of the "Labyrinth" is due to the influence of Andrea. "Andrea," he writes, "was

[1] De Quincy, in his "Historico-Critical Inquiry into the Origin of the Rosicrucians and Freemasons," has conjectured that Andrea himself was the originator, or at least the reviver, of that community. His armorial bearings—a St. Andrew's Cross and four roses—were undoubtedly their emblem.

[2] How little Komensky feared the accusation of plagiarism is proved by the fact that he gives the name of one of Andrea's books, "Fama Rosæorum," to one of the divisions of chapter xiii. This, according to the custom of the day, was equivalent to declaring the passage to be a quotation.

entirely pessimistic in his views, and even in his appearance resembled Schopenhauer." A more profound study of the life of Komensky would have rendered it very clear that Komensky—at least, the Komensky of the "Labyrinth"—became embittered through the circumstances of the time, and certainly required no foreign influence to strengthen such feeling. That Komensky, when writing school-books, wisely refrained from expressing such views is, I think, very natural; nor is it to the point that books written many years after the "Labyrinth" certainly tend to what is called optimism.

It is certain that when writing the "Labyrinth" Komensky wrote as a pessimist. That term has in recent years been used so largely and so vaguely that it may perhaps be as well to mention the sense in which I employ it. I consider that man a pessimist who believes that if we sum up the emotions and sensations of life in this world, we will find that those that are painful are both stronger and more numerous than those that are pleasurable. If we assume this standpoint, a man is neither more nor less a pessimist whether he believes that the joys of a future life will make good the horrors of the present one, or whether he longs for the quiet of Nirwana, or patiently awaits the absorption of his individuality in the totality of the world-soul. To prove that Komensky was a pessimist, it is sufficient to read the "Labyrinth" without the last chapters (xxxvii. to liv.), to which the author gave the separate name of the "Paradise of the Heart." Komensky, though eschewing theological controversy, writes as a devout Christian, and, indeed, member of the Unity. To Komensky (as I wrote some time ago), " it seemed that happiness, unattainable here, can be found elsewhere." This is, I think, the keynote of the " Labyrinth."

I have hitherto only referred to works that are earlier in date than the " Labyrinth"; but of all allegorical tales, the one that bears most resemblance to the " Labyrinth " is the " Pilgrim's Progress." [1] In both books a pilgrim passes through the evil world, with its great suffering and its many temptations. Evil guides lead astray both Komensky's and Bunyan's pilgrim, and both finally find perfect happiness and solace of their sorrows by means of God's grace. There are many minor resemblances—both books, for instance, contain a somewhat comic trial—that the reader will discover for himself. Yet there are great contrasts also between the two books, founded on the very different conditions of the writers. Bunyan knew only the tenets of his own community and the low life of his time. Komensky, on the other hand, had, at the time when he wrote the " Labyrinth,"

---

[1] It has been suggested to me that Bunyan may have had knowledge of the " Labyrinth," and that his words, " Some say the ' Pilgrim's Progress ' is not mine, insinuating as if I would shine, in name and fame, by the worth of another," refer to it. I consider this very improbable. There has, of course, never been an English translation of the " Labyrinth," and though Komensky may have mentioned his book during his stay in London, yet no information of this can well have reached Bunyan. Besides, as I have already stated, the idea on which both books are founded is far older than either of them.

travelled widely, studied at schools and universities, inquired into the latest theological and philosophical theories of his time, conferred with many learned men, and by means of his acquaintance with Charles of Zerotin, acquired some knowledge also of the life of the great of the world.

Bohemian writers have sought analogies to the "Labyrinth" among yet later writers, and have compared Goethe's "Wilhelm Meister's Lehr-und Wanderjahre" to Komensky's masterpiece. Such comparisons appear to me to be too far-fetched to require more than passing notice.

It may be well to give a brief outline of the "Labyrinth." The pilgrim, when arrived at that age "when the human mind begins to understand the difference between good and evil," starts on a voyage through the world to view it, and then "consider what group of men I should join, and with what matters occupy my life." The pilgrim is now joined by "Searchall" (called also "Impudence"), and afterwards by "Falsehood," evil guides that are servants of "Vanity, the queen of the world." By permission of "Fate, the lord regent of the queen," the pilgrim is allowed to enter the city of the world. He sees that it is "built in the shape of a circle," and is divided into countless streets, squares, houses, bigger and smaller buildings. The six principal streets are named according to the six principal professions, or "estates," as Komensky calls them, whose members dwell in them. They are the streets of the married people, the tradesmen, the scholars, the clergy, the magistrates and rulers, and lastly, the knights and warriors.

Bohemian writers have often remarked that these divisions appear somewhat arbitrary. It is, for instance, strange that matrimony should appear as an "estate" in distinction from other professions or callings. On the other hand, the reader is surprised that Komensky, writing in a country so largely agricultural as Bohemia, should not have mentioned the peasantry as one of the "estates." I venture a conjecture concerning this matter. The sympathy that Slavic writers—from Chelcicky to Count Tolstoy — have always expressed for the peasants, "the humble," is very evident in Komensky also. I need only refer to such passages in the "Labyrinth" as p. 306, when the writer refers to the cruel suffering that the Bohemian peasants underwent at the hands of the lords, and yet more of the overseers, whom the lords—often absentees—placed over them; and to the passage (p. 307) where the peasants receive the ironic answer to their complaints, "that if by willingness, compliance, and true attachment to their superiors and rulers, they could gain their favour, they should be allowed to enjoy it." As the main purpose of the earlier part of the "Labyrinth" is to prove that all professions are but vanity, and contain more evil than good, there was here no place for the peasants, who were humble by necessity, and had willingly or unwillingly to follow Komensky's precept, that it is better to obey than to rule.

After the pilgrim has passed twofold gates, he
beholds the various estates of mankind in the order
mentioned above. When dealing with matrimony,
Komensky expresses very pessimistic views, largely,
I think, to consistently maintain his theory that
everything earthly is evil ; for it may be mentioned
here that Komensky, who became a widower in
1622, married again in 1624, and after losing his
second wife, married again late in life.

The pilgrim now comes to the street of the
tradesmen, and Komensky's descriptions here throw
a great deal of light on the dangerous and laborious
life then led by those who were employed in trade
and the transport of merchandise. The waggoners
underwent many hardships, and the fate of the sailors
was yet worse. Very picturesque is the description
of a sea voyage and subsequent shipwreck. It is
founded on the author's experiences during his
journey to England, and is therefore a later
addition, which we first meet with in the edition
of the "Labyrinth" published at Amsterdam in 1663.
Komensky's comparison of the different parts of
a waggon to the different parts of a ship is one
of the many quaint conceits that render the
"Labyrinth" so attractive.

The pilgrim then visits the scholars or learned
men. His descriptions of school-life, written from
his own experiences, are very distressing. Plagosus
Orbilius had at that time many imitators in the
Bohemian schools. The pilgrim then pursues his
journey through the halls of higher learning, and
his visit to the scholars is indeed described with

far more detail than that to any of the other
"streets." The pilgrim visits consecutively the
philosophers—here Komensky gives a curious list
of philosophers founded on Andrea—the grammarians, rhetoricians, and poets. The writer
violently attacks the heathen poets of Greece and
Rome, whom, indeed, in his capacity as a pedagogue,
he afterwards wished to expel from the schools
and replace by Christian writers. Fortunately,
from the point of view of classical scholarship, this
attempt failed. The pilgrim, or rather Komensky,
then visits the dwellings of those who teach the
various other branches of learning, delivering short,
and sometimes sharp, criticisms on the scientific
theories that were current in his day. Sometimes
he deals, with veiled irony, of matters also that are
now no longer considered subjects of scientific
research, such as the quadrature of the circle, the
philosopher's stone, astrology and alchemy. As
regards alchemy,[1] we must, however, remember that
it was considered by learned men a subject worthy
of serious study, even many years after the
"Labyrinth" was written.

The pilgrim next visits the street of the clergy.
After referring briefly to the Jews and Mohamme-
dans, Komensky devotes a long chapter (chap.
xvii.) to the Christian creed. The comparative
tolerance shown here to views different from those

[1] In 1667, Spinoza entered into a correspondence with some
friends on the subject of alchemy. "He was obviously disposed to think seriously of the matter [i.e., alchemy] at that
time."—Sir F. Pollock, "Spinoza," p. 62. It is but fair to add
that Spinoza's views on this subject afterwards changed.

of the writer deserves notice, though it is always evident that his sympathy is with the "true Christians," as he terms the members of the Unity. Komensky's diatribe against unworthy priests and bishops, " who wear a coat of mail over a surplice, a helmet over a barat; who hold the Word of God in one hand, a sword in the other; who carry Peter's keys in front, and Judas's wallet behind; whose mind is educated by Scripture, though their heart is practised in fraud; whose tongue is full of piety, though their eyes are full of wantonness," will, at the present day, appear offensive to the members of no Christian community. Komensky's conception of Christianity, as a vast church that has many side-chapels for those who profess the various Christian doctrines, is one of the finest allegories in a book in which fine allegories are frequent.

The pilgrim's path next leads him among the magistrates and rulers. The trial of Simplicity before the judges is very quaint, and proves that Komensky was by no means devoid of humour. The names of some of the judges, such as Lovegold, Takegift, Loveself, remind the reader of Bunyan.

After the magistrates, the pilgrim visits the rulers. They have neither eyes nor ears nor tongue, and communicate with their subjects by means of tubes. Komensky thus describes satirically the difficulty which a humble man encounters when he endeavours to approach the rulers, who see, hear, and speak only through their courtiers and councillors.

The pilgrim is now conducted to the street of the soldiers and knights. Here the intense hatred of bloodshed and warfare, so characteristic of the brethren, is very evident. The battle-piece (chap. xx.) has rightly been admired as one of the most striking and eloquent things that Komensky ever wrote. Of the knights, Komensky writes somewhat briefly. His writings show that he shared the detestation of coats-of-arms, and all hereditary dignities, that was characteristic of his community, from Chelcicky [1] (indirectly its founder) downward. It is scarcely doubtful that Komensky dealt but superficially with this matter, to show well-deserved courtesy to Charles, lord of Zerotin, under whose protection he then resided at Brandeis, and to whom the "Labyrinth" is dedicated. Charles of Zerotin, a great statesman and a great Bohemian writer,[2] was indeed, as regards his fame, by no means dependent on the glory of his ancestors. Yet even a far-seeing and enlightened nobleman like Zerotin, to whom Komensky's short and severe account of knightly life was in no way applicable, would perhaps have resented sharper attacks on the knights and nobles of his country.

Having now found but vanity and vileness in the six principal streets of the city of the world, the pilgrim, still conducted by his guides, Searchall

[1] For Chelcicky, see my "History of Bohemian Literature," pp. 153-157, and particularly pp. 159-171. I have there translated part of Chelcicky's fiercely satirical attack on the armorial bearings of the Bohemian nobles.

[2] For Charles of Zerotin, see my "History of Bohemian Literature," pp. 321-325.

and Falsehood, proceeds in the direction of the Castle of Fortune. The guides tell him that those who have in their estates struggled successfully in the city here enjoy perfect comfort and all pleasures. A curious intermezzo occurs here; near the lower gate of the castle the pilgrim meets the " newsmen "—it would be an anachronism to call them journalists—they carry whistles, on which they pipe different and discordant notes, some cheerful, some melancholy.

To the castle, one principal gate, that of virtue, leads; but it is difficult of access, and little frequented. There are also several side-entrances, which have various names such as Hypocrisy, Injustice, Violence, and so forth. Even those who have passed through the outward barriers are not all allowed to ascend to the castle itself. This depends on the caprice of Fortune, who lifts upward on her wheel those who find favour with her. The castle itself has three floors, in which the rich, the voluptuous, and the famous men dwell. The pilgrim first visits the rich, whom he finds hugging their chains, which they believe to be golden. He then ascends to the banquet hall of the revellers. Komensky here gives an incident of a truly comic character. The pilgrim is at first horrified by the behaviour of the banqueters, whom he leaves after having severely rebuked them. He is, however, induced by his guides to return, and joins in the revels—but too freely! He then arrives at the dwelling-places of the famous men, who have achieved immortality; but he is disappointed here also, for among those whose fame will endure for ever he finds Herostratus.

The pilgrim, finding the labours and the joys of the world equally vain and distasteful, now begins to despair; but his guides comfort him by telling him that they will lead him to the palace of the Queen of Wisdom—which is really that of worldly wisdom or vanity. He finds the queen surrounded by numerous councillors and guards, who bear fantastic allegorical names. His guides then accuse him before the queen of being "anxious, disgusted with all things, and desirous of something unusual."

The queen none the less receives the pilgrim graciously, and invites him to remain in her palace, where he hopes henceforth to live in peace. Meanwhile, Solomon, accompanied by a large following, consisting of philosophers and scholars of all countries, arrives at the queen's court, and claims her in marriage. The queen answers through "Prudence, her councillor," that "Wisdom was the spouse of God alone, and could wed no other." Solomon, however, remains at her court, and in his presence and that of his followers the queen receives numerous deputations of nobles, scholars, jurisconsults, labourers, and others. These petitions, and the replies given to them—like the pilgrim's visits to the streets of the world, and afterwards to the dwellers in the Castle of Fortune—throw a strong and clear light on many circumstances connected with the social and political life of Bohemia and Germany in the early years of the seventeenth century. They have, therefore, considerable value for those who study this period.

On the other hand, it must be admitted that many of the grievances and complaints contained in these passages of the "Labyrinth" are world-old, belong to all times, and will, no doubt, endure for ever. Men will always enlarge on the hardships of those who seek fortune, the pedantry and credulity of scholars, the "odium theologicum" so great among those who teach the doctrine of peace and goodwill, the brutality of the soldiery, the injustice of judges, "the law's delay, the insolence of office."

But to return to the pilgrim. He had been listening to the speeches of the deputations, with the other members of the queen's Court, when the audiences are suddenly interrupted. Incensed by the deceitful decrees of the queen, Solomon exclaims with a loud voice : " Vanity of vanities, and all is vanity ! " He then tears the mask from the face of the queen, and she, who had previously seemed beautiful, now appears as a hideous hag. Solomon and his followers leave the queen's palace, and hurrying to the city of the world, they loudly proclaim the vanity of all earthly things. The queen is at first terrified by Solomon's invective, but soon recovers her senses, and assembles all her councillors, asking them to advise her how she can best expel Solomon from her dominions. Some advise the arming of all the queen's forces, but others suggest that the queen should employ craft rather than violence ; at least, at first. The latter

counsel prevails.   Three of the queen's companions,
Flattery, Affability, and Pleasure, follow Solomon
into the city of the world, and entice him into the
street of the married people.   His follies there are
described in a manner that very closely follows the
Biblical account.   The queen now decides to attack
Solomon, who has been deserted by many of his
followers.   A fearful massacre ensues, and the
terrified pilgrim exclaims: " O God, if Thou art a
God, have mercy on wretched me! " and he then
swoons.

We have now reached the second part of the
" Labyrinth," to which Komensky has given the
name of the " Paradise of the Heart."   Henceforth
everything is changed; all sordid, and sometimes
coarse, allusions to worldly matters vanish, and we
find ourselves in an atmosphere of purest mysticism.
Christ appears to the pilgrim and welcomes him
home—that is to say, as one who, from his earthly
wandering, has returned to the solitude of his
heart.   He then receives Christ as a guest in his
humble dwelling, and they are mystically betrothed.
Christ informs the pilgrim that he is one of those
whom He has chosen, and gives him instructions as
to his behaviour during the time that he will yet
remain upon earth.   These instructions are, of
course, entirely in accordance with the teaching of
the Bohemian brethren, the community to which
Komensky belonged.

Though yet remaining on earth, the pilgrim now
beholds the splendour of heaven in a vision, and
sees God on a throne of jasper, surrounded by the

hosts of the angels. The influence of the Apocalypse is here very evident. Komensky, as all the " brethren " of his time, was an indefatigable student of Scripture. The " Bible of Kralice," to which I have already referred, was always in their hands, and the " Labyrinth " shows many traces of its study. Komensky's vision of heaven is very striking, and I do not hesitate to say that it has sometimes reminded me of Dante's " Paradise."

After the vision has disappeared, the pilgrim falls on his knees and addresses to God a prayer, breathing that passionate and disinterested love of the divinity that is so characteristic of the mystics. With this chapter the book ends. But in this chapter, as in several others, such as that which deals with the pilgrim's mystical betrothal with Christ, we are carried upward to the highest summits of mystic thought. Had the book been written in a language better known than that of Bohemia, it would, I think, have ranked high among the works belonging to that school of thought. It would be interesting to examine to what extent Komensky was influenced by the writings of the German mystics, but limited space renders this impossible.

Though the " Labyrinth " is, to a certain extent, a philosophical work, and, to a certain extent, also a book of adventure, yet it must be considered as mainly a theological work. It could not be otherwise as regards a book written by Komensky, who called himself " hominem vocatione theologum," and who, in all his writings, even on other subjects,

referred constantly to theological matters. Thus,
in his "pansophic works," philosophy is still the
handmaiden of theology, an idea that even in his
days was already becoming obsolete.

If we consider at what time and under what
circumstances the "Labyrinth" was written, we
shall be surprised to find how little religious controversy and "odium theologicum" it contains. If
we except a brief allusion[1] to the cruelty with
which the Church of Rome enforced its doctrine,
there is in the book no attack even on that Church
that was then cruelly persecuting the brethren.
The more enlightened Catholics have not failed
to recognise this. The learned Bohemian Jesuit
Balbinus,[2] wrote in his "Bohemia Docta":
"Komensky wrote very many works, but none that
were aimed at the Catholic Church. When reading his works, it has always appeared to me that
he wrote with great prudence, as if he did not wish
to show preference to any religious doctrine, nor
condemn any." In the present century also the
historian, Dr. Gindely, a writer of pronounced
Catholic views, has declared that some of the works
of Komensky are as those of a saint. That in spite
of these enlightened judgments, both temporal and
ecclesiastical authorities have several times attempted to suppress the "Labyrinth" has already
been mentioned. The teaching of Komensky is
that of the "Unity," which insisted mainly on a
holy life, and advised the brethren to live secluded

[1] Chapter xviii. 15.
[2] Born, 1621; died, 1688.

lives; to eschew as far as possible worldly honours; to obey, rather than to command; in short, to conform as closely as they could to the ways of the first disciples and followers of Christ. Leaving all doctrinal considerations aside, it cannot be denied that this was a lofty ideal.

On controversial matters, Komensky, in the "Labyrinth," is significantly silent. As Dr. von Criegern writes, even the questions of free will and predestination that divided the Lutherans and Calvinists, to which communities the brethren were closely related, though they belonged to neither, Komensky devoted little attention. There are, however, several passages in the last chapters of the "Labyrinth" (the "Paradise of the Heart") that afford some evidence in favour of the author's belief in predestination. I have already referred to the mysticism of the "Labyrinth." The mystic conception of light is very prominent in the book, and is occasionally rather puzzling to the reader, as the word appears sometimes in its ordinary, sometimes in its allegorical, signification. The conception of Christ as "the centre of all things" is also common to many mystics, as is the great stress laid on various odours, as the reader will find in many passages of the "Labyrinth." M. Nordau would, no doubt, on the strength of this peculiarity, enrol Komensky among the "Entartete"; it is, however, true that mysticism itself is degeneracy, according to M. Nordau.

I have already written much on Komensky's

life,[1] but I think the readers of the " Labyrinth "
will wish to find here a short account of the long
and eventful life of its author.   I shall do this as
briefly as possible, except when dealing with
Komensky's stay at Brandeis, where he wrote the
" Labyrinth."

John Amos Komensky [2] was born in 1592 at
Uhersky Brod,[3] a small town in Moravia.   He lost
his parents when quite young, and received his
earliest education at Uhersky Brod, at the school
that the brethren had established there.   His
family had long belonged to that community.
Komensky's experiences at school were very painful.   The almost inconceivable brutality of the
teachers of that day, who looked down on corporal
punishment not merely as a penalty for offences,
but as a measure that was likely to stimulate the
minds of the young to intellectual efforts, deeply
impressed   the   high-strung   nature   of   young
Komensky.   He has alluded to his school-days
in the " Labyrinth " (chap. x.), and there is little
doubt that the recollection of his early experiences
influenced him when he endeavoured later in life
to amend the educational system.   After leaving

[1] I have referred to it briefly in my " Bohemia : an Historical
Sketch," and more fully in my "History of Bohemian
Literature."

[2] According to the latest researches, the name of Komensky's
family was originally Milic ; they adopted the name of
Komensky (Latinised to Comenius) when they settled in
the little village of Komna, in Moravia.   Komensky's father
afterwards moved from there to the neighbouring town of
Uhersky Brod.

[3] *I.e.*, " The ford of the Hungarians."

Uherský Brod, Komensky spent some time at the school of the Unity at Prerov (Prerau), also in Moravia, and then proceeded to the Calvinist University at Herborn, in Nassau. That university, founded in the sixteenth century by Henry, Count of Nassau, was then one of the strongholds of the Calvinist creed. The brethren often sent their promising pupils who were to become clergymen to that university, rather to the then utrafuist [1] University of Prague. It is certain that Komensky's views, particularly early in life, show traces of his Calvinistic training. From Herborn, Komensky proceeded to Heidelberg, then the residence of Frederick of the Palatinate, destined shortly afterwards to become the "winterking" of Bohemia. Though we have little positive information on the matter, he seems to have travelled extensively at this period, to have visited the Netherlands and Amsterdam, which was to be the refuge of his last years.

Komensky returned to his own country in 1614, and was appointed a minister of his Church in 1616, with residence in the small town of Fulneck, in Moravia. He married there, and spent a few peaceful years, the happiest of his long life.

But even a pious preacher and teacher could not

[1] *I.e.,* receiving Communion in both kinds (subutraque). This was the official designation of all those not Romanists who, up to the battle of the White Mountain, enjoyed religious freedom in Bohemia. The old utrafuist teachings, such as then prevailed at the University of Prague, differed but little, except on this one point, from the teaching of Rome; and the more advanced reformers therefore preferred to send their youths to foreign universities.

long remain untouched by the vicissitudes of the
Thirty Years' War, and the unspeakable horrors
that befell Bohemia and Moravia after the battle
of the White Mountain in 1620. In the following year, Spanish troops, that came as allies of
Ferdinand II., German Emperor and Archduke of
Austria, attacked the small town of Fulneck. The
town was captured without resistance. Here, as
almost everywhere at that time, the inhabitants
immediately submitted to the victorious Romanists.
Komensky's house was pillaged and burnt down,
and—to him almost a greater loss—his library and
MSS. also perished in the flames. Komensky fled
to Bohemia with his wife and children, and sought
refuge with Charles, Lord of Zerotin, at Brandeis
on the Orlice.[1] I have already mentioned the name
of Charles of Zerotin. During the war that had
just ended he had, though a fervent Bohemian
patriot and member of the Unity, not espoused
the cause of Frederick of the Palatinate, but had
remained faithful to the House of Habsburg. It
was therefore natural that the victors showed
him a certain amount of consideration. His vast
estates were not confiscated by the Austrian
Government, and he was allowed to remain in
the dominions of the House of Habsburg. He
was even tacitly, though by no means officially,
granted yet further privileges ; he was allowed
to afford at least temporary shelter to some of
the clergymen of his Church, whom one of the

---

[1] In German, "Adler."

first decrees of the victors had expelled from
Bohemia.

Komensky, as I have already mentioned, was
one of those who availed themselves of the
hospitality of Zerotin. As far as the rather uncertain accounts inform us, he did not live in the
town of Brandeis, but in a cottage on the opposite
bank of the Orlice, at the foot of the hill still
called "Klopota." This is confirmed by the fact
that Komensky has thus signed his Latin dedication of the "Labyrinth" to his patron: "Dabam
sub Klopot Idibus, Dec. 1623." According to very
old traditions, the wooden cottage or hut (the
Bohemian "chalupa") in which he lived was of
very ancient origin, having been built with his
own hands by Brother Gregory,[1] one of the
founders of the Unity.

Brandeis, on the Orlice, which will always be
memorable to all Bohemians as the spot where
Komensky wrote the "Labyrinth," was then
already holy ground for a member of the
Unity. It had been one of the earliest settle-
ments of the brethren, and for a long time the
dwelling-place of Brother Gregory, who had first
organised the community. Here, too, Brother
Gregory had died (in 1474), and had been buried,
"like the prophets of the Old Testament, in a
rock-grave near the bank of the Orlice—that is
to say, opposite the castle."[2] The owners of

[1] For Brother Gregory, see my "History of Bohemian
Literature," pp. 203, 205, 207, etc.
[2] Dr. Goll.

Brandeis—the lords of Postupic, and afterwards the lords of Zerotin—had always been well disposed towards the Bohemian brethren ; the Zerotins, indeed, belonged to the Unity. It was, therefore, natural that Brandeis should have been frequently chosen as meeting-place for the synods of the community of which it had become the centre.

When Komensky arrived at Brandeis, about the end of the year 1622, he was overwhelmed with misery to a degree, that only his true Christian faith and his thorough reliance on the doctrine of his community enabled him to overcome. As already mentioned, all his worldly possessions—including his beloved books and MSS.—had perished. Perished also had all prospects of a successful career as a clergyman and pedagogue, at least in his beloved native country, for Komensky well knew that of all "acatholics," [1] the members of the Unity would be the first to be expelled from Bohemia. During the lengthy and dangerous journey from Fulneck to Brandeis, undertaken at a time of pestilence and in the midst of the horrors of the Thirty Years' War, Komensky lost his wife and one of his children ; the other died shortly after his arrival at Brandeis. It was not, therefore, as one influenced by temporary irritation or disappointment, but as one who " bears the whole heaviness of the wronged

---

[1] This, up to comparatively recent times, was the official designation in Austria of all who did not belong to the Church of Rome.

world's weight," that Komensky wrote the
" Labyrinth."

Believers in Taine's theory of "milieu" will
certainly be strengthened in their belief if they
visit Brandeis after reading the "Labyrinth." The
little town nestles at the banks of the rapid, grey,
dolorous Orlice. The narrow valley in which the
town is situated is encircled, and, as it were,
weighed down by never-ending pine-forests that
rise abruptly in all directions, but particularly in
that of the Klopota Hill, under which Komensky's
hut stood. This spot, memorable as being the one
where he conceived the "Labyrinth," is now marked
by a small monument erected to him by his grateful countrymen. Straight before him, separated
only by the Orlice, stood the city of Brandeis, with
its wide market-place, to which all the small
streets converged. Immediately behind the town
stood, as a "Castle of Fortune," the ancient castle
of the Zerotins, then already a ruin. Situated on
a steep and abrupt rock, it so entirely overlooks
the town that the traveller can see directly beneath
him the market-place "crowded with people as
with insects." This is particularly the case during
the summer months, for Brandeis has now become
a fashionable summer resort of the citizens of
Prague.

It is, of course, as a mere conjecture that I
venture to suggest that Komensky had the city of
Brandeis and the neighbouring scenery in his
mind when he wrote the "Labyrinth." Such con-
jectures have not, perhaps, great value, even when

made by one who has been a constant wanderer in the district referred to. Similar attempts to connect great writings with the scenery that surrounded their author while he wrote them have often been made; and it is certain that a man of genius—such as Komensky undoubtedly was—would be more strongly impressed and influenced by the scenery around him than an ordinary man.

Meanwhile, Komensky's stay in his beloved Bohemia was drawing to an end. The condition of the brethren at Brandeis was at first a fairly tolerable one. The Austrian Government, grateful to Zerotin for his fidelity to the house of Habsburg, did not at first molest his protégés much. But the position of non-Catholics became more precarious in the Habsburg dominions every year. Every year the regulations against them became more severe. Komensky, like many of the brethren, lived in secrecy, and only occasionally returned to Brandeis. At last the brethren, among whom was Komensky, decided, at a secret meeting in the village of Doubravic, that they would altogether abandon Bohemia, and settle in Poland and Hungary. It was also agreed to that certain members of the community should precede the general emigration, and seek in these countries places of refuge where the brethren could continue to worship freely according to their doctrine. Komensky was chosen as one of these envoys, and now travelled extensively in Northern Germany and Poland. It was decided that Komensky and other brethren should seek refuge at Lesno or Lissa,[1] in Poland, under the protection of Count Lescynski, who was himself a member of their community. It was during these travels that Komensky first became acquainted with the so-called "prophecies" of Kotter and Eliza Ponatovska; together with the later "prophecies" of Drabik, they had a great influence on Komensky in his later years. There is, however, little trace of their influence in the "Labyrinth,"[2] so that it is unnecessary to refer to them here.[3]

In January, 1628, Komensky, accompanied by several other exiles, left Bohemia—that he was never destined to revisit. When the exiles arrived at the Silesian frontier, "they all knelt down and prayed to God, with cries and many tears, entreating Him not finally to avert His mercy from their beloved country, nor to allow the seed of His word to perish within it."[4]

On the 8th of February, Komensky arrived at Lissa. He spent there a considerable number of years conscientiously fulfilling his duties, both as preacher and schoolmaster of the small Bohemian community that had settled there. It was at this time that he wrote many of his educational works

---

[1] In the present Prussian province of Posen.

[2] See, however, note 1, p. 393, chap. xlvii.

[3] The influence of these "prophets" on Komensky has great, though very painful, psychological interest. I have referred to them in my "History of Bohemian Literature," as mentioned in the note to chapter xlvii. referred to above. There is a fuller account of Kotter's "prophecies" in my "Bohemia : an Historical Sketch," pp. 396-398.

[4] Zoubek, "Zivot Komenského."

that, to a certain extent, preserved his fame, even when he was least known. Thus a large part of the "Didactica Magna" was written at Lissa. Here, also, Komensky began his pansophic studies at this time, and his first philosophical (or pansophic) book appeared in 1632. Though written during the troublous times of the Thirty Years' War, Komensky's pansophic studies attracted great attention. Indeed, the horrors of that war may have inclined the minds of men to that mysticism that promised them a delightful future, contrasting with the wretched present. It is always in times of great misery that mystic, particularly chiliastic, ideas, such as Komensky professed in the last years of his life, appeal most to the minds of men.

The interest in Komensky's pansophic studies was not limited to Poland, Bohemia, and Germany. His fame spread also to far more distant countries' particularly to England, that did not interfere in the thirty years' struggle on the Continent, but that was then on the verge of civil war. Samuel Hartlib, well known as a friend of Milton, was greatly interested in the studies of the Bohemian pansophist. A correspondence began between Hartlib and Komensky, to whom Hartlib offered financial aid to enable him to visit England. After some hesitation, Komensky accepted this offer. His temporary hope of returning to Bohemia—founded on the brilliant victories of Gustavus Adolphus—had proved vain. Count Lescynski, his old patron, had died, and shortly afterwards his son had, for political reasons, adopted the creed of Rome.

Other causes contributed to render Komensky less desirous of remaining at Lissa. He had not, in his later writings, always shown that generous, large-minded, truly Christian tolerance that is so conspicuous in the "Labyrinth," and was already becoming involved in those theological controversies that afterwards embittered his last years. Discord appears to have arisen between him and other clergymen of the community of Lissa, though the fact that he was chosen as the head of that community seven years later proves that he had by no means lost its sympathy.

In the summer of 1641, Komensky left Lissa on his way to England. He arrived in London on September 21, after a very perilous sea voyage, of which he has left us a description in the "Labyrinth."[1] I have elsewhere referred to Komensky's stay in London, and to the very interesting letter dealing mainly with English affairs that he sent to his friends on the Continent. He seems to have been acquainted with many men of importance in England. Besides Hartlib, on whose invitation he had come there, Theodore Haak, John Durie, John Beale, Evelyn were among those whom Komensky met in London. It is less certain that he made the personal acquaintance of Milton and of Lord Herbert of Cherbury.[2]

[1] This, of course, does not appear in the first edition of the "Labyrinth." It is first printed in the edition of the book published at Amsterdam in 1663.

[2] That Komensky corresponded with Lord Herbert is proved by his correspondence, recently published by Mr. Patera. It contains a letter dated June 15, 1647, addressed

It is not my intention to refer here in more detail to the Bohemian philosopher's stay in London, where he and his friends wished to found a pansophic academy. Public events in England rendered such an undertaking an impossibility.

Komensky therefore decided to leave London, and started, in June, 1642, only a few weeks before civil war broke out in England. Through Holland and Germany, he proceeded to Sweden. He had been invited to that country by the Chancellor Oxenstierna, who had heard of his fame as an educator from Louis de Geer, a rich Dutch merchant, who had business connection with Sweden. Oxenstierna wished Komensky to undertake the task of writing a series of school-books for use in the Swedish schools. Komensky consented to do so, but refused to take up his residence in Sweden. He settled for some time (1642-1648) at Elbing, a small—now Prussian—town on the Baltic, not very distant from the Swedish coast. Conscientious as he always was, he worked hard there at the school-books he had undertaken to write, while he also laboured hard at his pansophic works, encouraged by his English friends, who urged him not to devote all his time to "mere school-books."

to the "Perillustri atque noblissimo Domino, Domino Edwardo Baroni Herbert de Cherbury, etc., etc. Domino et Fautori meo." Komensky here thanks Herbert for the gift of the volume, "De Causis Errorum": "Tam gratum quam flagranter desideratum munus," as he calls it. From the time of his visit to England, Komensky frequently mentions Lord Herbert's name when writing to his English friends.

Komensky's stay at Elbing ended in 1648. In that year Justinus, bishop of the Unity, died at Lissa, and Komensky was chosen as his successor. He did not hesitate to accept that dignity, a heavy burden at a moment when the Treaty of Westphalia had destroyed the last hopes of the brethren, and the community seemed doomed to extinction. He started in the same year for Lissa, to assume the duties of his new office.

But here also he did not now remain long. He was summoned to Transylvania by George Rakoczy, who was then ruler of that country, and of a considerable part of Hungary. Rakoczy, a Calvinist, was naturally anxious to obtain the services of one whose creed was very similar to his own, and who already was far famed as an educator. Komensky stayed some time at Potok,[1] where the princes of the house of Rakoczy often resided. In consequence of the favour that he enjoyed with these princes, he was able to carry out his educational innovations here on a much larger scale than before. His labours at Potok have therefore great value for those interested in pedagogy,[2] but it is unnecessary to refer to them here.

In 1654, Komensky returned for the last time to Lissa, but only for a brief period. He was destined soon to become a wanderer again. War broke out in 1655 between Poland and Sweden, and the

---

[1] A town in Northern Hungary. Its Hungarian name is Saros-Patak.

[2] There is an interesting account of Komensky's organisation of the Hungarian schools in Dr. Kvacsala's (German) "Johann Amos Comenius."

Bohemian exiles, though they had been well treated by the Poles, sympathised largely with the Swedes, whose Protestantism was somewhat similar to their own. Komensky, far too great an enthusiast to be a cautious man, shared this feeling, and gave utterance to it in his "Panegyricus Carolo Gustavo magno Suecorum regi." The Swedes were at first victorious, overran a large part of Poland, and captured the town of Lissa. In 1656, however, the Poles recaptured the town and completely destroyed it, partly, as Komensky's enemies alleged, because of his panegyric on the King of Sweden. Komensky's library and MSS. were for a second time destroyed. He, now already sixty-five years old, found himself again a homeless wanderer. After staying some time at Stettin, Hamburg, and other places, he at last found a refuge at Amsterdam. Lawrence de Geer, the son of his old patron, Louis de Geer, invited him to reside there. It was there that Komensky spent the last years of his troubled life. His chiliastic views, and his firm belief in so-called "prophets," involved him in much theological controversy, carried on with the discourtesy, and indeed brutality, customary among the theologians of his time. Many false or exaggerated accusations against Komensky, gathered from the controversial writings of his opponents, were afterwards repeated by Bayle in his "Dictionnaire Historique et Critique," and Komensky was long principally judged according to Bayle's one-sided account. The greater interest now shown in Komensky's educational work, and, on the other hand, the revival of Bohemian literature, which has made a book such as the " Labyrinth " better known, have caused the great Bohemian writer to be now judged more fairly.

Komensky's last years were very melancholy ; his old friends and comrades, Gertych, Figulus (his son-in-law), and other clergymen of the Unity, died, and he became more and more solitary. He doubtlessly believed that the community to which he had devoted his whole life would perish from the earth. This was not, however, to be the case ; Komensky's grandson, Figulus, or Jablonsky, as he generally called himself, consecrated as a clergyman of the Unity Count Zinzendorf, the founder of the community of Herrenhut, that has continued to the present day, and which in its principal doctrines is identical with the old community,[1] occupied to the last with pansophic studies. Komensky died at Amsterdam on November 15, 1670. An exile even in death, he was buried on November 22 in the Church of the French Protestants at Naarden, near Amsterdam.

After what has necessarily been a very slight sketch of Komensky's career, I return to the " Labyrinth." Not to give too terrifying an aspect to the title-page of this book, I have given on it

[1] The learned deacon of Herrenhut, Dr. J. Muller, has dealt with the connection of his community with the old brethren in a series of very interesting studies, published in the *Casopis Musea Kralovstoi* (Journal of the Bohemian Museum) for 1885. He says that though there are minor differences, the teaching of his community is on all important points identical with that of the old Unity.

only the first principal part of the name that
Komensky chose for his work. It may, however,
be interesting to give here the full name, which,
according to the fashion of the day, is very lengthy.
Komensky thus describes his book: "The Labyrinth of the World and the Paradise¹ of the
Heart; that is, a book that clearly shows that this
world and all matters concerning it are nothing but
confusion and giddiness, pain and toil, deceit and
falsehood, misery and anxiety, and lastly, disgust
of all things and despair; but he who remains in
his own dwelling within his heart, opening it to the
Lord God alone, will obtain true and full peace of
mind and joy."

Following the example of all former editors of
Komensky's masterpiece, I have made no external
distinction between the "Labyrinth of the World"
and the "Paradise of the Heart." Komensky
himself made no such distinction, and here also the
chapters are numbered continuously, as they are in
the Amsterdam edition of 1663. It has often been
stated that the "Paradise," which is much shorter
than the "Labyrinth," is also inferior to it. It is
certain that while a large, and perhaps the most
interesting part of the "Labyrinth," describes the
customs and manner of life of the six "estates"
into which Komensky divides mankind, the lives of
the same classes of men are described, but in a few

¹ In the first edition, the word "Lusthauz," derived from
the German, is used. In the Amsterdam edition, and all the
subsequent ones, the correct Bohemian word "Raj" is
employed.

words after they have become "true Christians," a
term which, to Komensky, always meant a member
of the Unity. Yet such criticism is founded on
an inadequate conception of Komensky's purpose
when he wrote the "Labyrinth." It was not his
intention to extol earthly life, even that of the
most God-fearing pietist, but to enlarge on the
vileness of the world, and to contrast with it the
perfect happiness of those who in heaven are united
with God.

Though Komensky's works, and the "Labyrinth"—his masterpiece—in particular, have been
the object of much interest since the revival of
Bohemian literature, yet a critical study of the
"Labyrinth," dealing fully with all philological,
historical, artistic, and other questions connected
with it, is still a desideratum. It is not, therefore,
yet quite certain what chapters of the "Labyrinth"
formed part of the book as first written, and what
are later editions. Dr. Flajshans, in his excellent
"Pisemnictvi Ceske," (*i.e.* Bohemian Literature)
suggests that chapters xxix. to xxxv. did not form
part of the book as written at Brandeis, though
they already appear in the first printed edition of
1631. The description of a shipwreck in chapter
viii., founded on Komensky's own experience, first
appears in the Amsterdam edition of 1663.

It may be of interest to refer to the various
editions and translations of the "Labyrinth."
They are by no means numerous, if we consider the
value of the book. It must, however, be remembered that the suppression of Komensky's creed in

his country followed its appearance very closely,
and that the Bohemian language in which it is
written was, for a time, almost extinct. Though
finished in 1623, the book, as already mentioned, was
first printed in 1631.[1] A second enlarged edition
appeared at Amsterdam in 1663. After this there
was no new edition before 1757,[2] when the book was
reprinted at Berlin. Further editions appeared at
Prague in 1782 and 1809. The latter edition,
though it had appeared with the consent of the
" censure,"[3] which then decided what books might
be printed in Austria and Bohemia, was yet suppressed in 1820, and the " Labyrinth," for a time,
again became almost inaccessible to Komensky's
countrymen. Since the accession of that enlightened ruler, the present Emperor of Austria, Francis
Joseph, these petty molestations have ceased. The
" Labyrinth " has been frequently reprinted, and is
now in the hands of all Bohemian readers, who
have the same affection for the book that their
ancestors had more than two centuries ago. In
consequence of Komensky's great mastery of his
language, parts of the " Labyrinth " are read in the
Bohemian schools, in which the national language
is now largely used. It is not necessary to
enumerate the many editions of the " Labyrinth "
that have appeared within the last years. The

[1] According to Mr. Bily, probably either at Lissa or at
Pirna, in Saxony.

[2] There is a copy of this edition in the library of the British
Museum.

[3] See my " History of Bohemian Literature," passim,
particularly pp. 366-369, and 397-398.

best is that published in the present year by Mr.
Bily. I have consulted it for those parts of the
"Labyrinth" also that I had translated before the
appearance of Mr. Bily's edition. It follows very
closely the Amsterdam edition of 1663, and has
some valuable notes, of which I have availed
myself on several occasions. I must here also
acknowledge my indebtedness to Dr. Kvacsala's
"Johann Amos Comenius," Dr. Zoubek's "Zivot
Komenského," (*i.e.*, "Life of Komensky"), Professor
Kapras's "Nástin Filosophie Komenského, (*i.e.*,
"Outline of Komensky's Philosophy"), Dr. von
Criegern's "Comenius als Theolog," and numerous
studies in the Casopis Musea Ceského (*i.e.*, "Journal of the Bohemian Museum "). Of those essays, I
should particularly mention those of Dr. Novak on
the "Labyrinth of the World," that appeared in
the Journal in 1895. It would be unnecessary
to give a full list of the authorities consulted, as
these books are almost all written in the Bohemian
language that is practically unknown in England.

The causes, already mentioned, that limited
the number of editions of the "Labyrinth" also
account for the fact that the book has not been
more frequently translated into foreign languages.
An abridged German translation was published at
Potsdam in 1781, and another translation, or rather
adaptation, appeared at Berlin in 1787 under the
name of "Philosophisch Satirische Reisen durch
alle Stände der menschlichen Handlungen." The
latest German translation was published in 1871 or
1872; the book has no date. This translation,

published at Spremberg by Dr. Novotny, a Protestant divine, has little or no value. The translator, who evidently had but a slight knowledge of the Bohemian language, has made some rather serious mistakes; he has also, with an audacity that would appear inconceivable on the part of one translating from a better known language than that of Bohemia, omitted considerable passages of the "Labyrinth," while he has inserted a good deal of matter that is not contained in Komensky's MS. There are also Hungarian and Russian translations of the "Labyrinth."

In his preface to the "Labyrinth," Komensky tells his reader "that it is not a poem that you will read, although it may have the seeming of a poem." I have explained in a note what I believe to be Komensky's meaning. Yet the author may also have intended to point out to his readers that his book was written in a somewhat ornate manner, differing largely from the rather homely prose that was then usual in Bohemia. It is, I think, the first duty of a translator to render as closely and faithfully as he can the word and thought of the author whose writings he endeavours to transfer into a different language; he should, therefore, adhere as closely as possible not only to the current of thought, but even to the manner of writing of his author. I have therefore not hesitated in using some words that at the present day are hardly used in English prose, and in employing some rather archaic locutions. Such locutions would, of course, not have appeared so unusual to Komensky's contemporaries in England than they may to the readers of the present day. Komensky, particularly in the "Labyrinth," uses alliteration to a great extent. As far as the totally different character of the English and Bohemian languages permitted, I have endeavoured to follow him in this also.

I must also, writing in a language that is not my own, beg my readers' indulgence to such lapses from the now most usual methods of writing English that may be found in this translation.

It is scarcely necessary to mention that a God-fearing and pious man, such as was Komensky, admitted nothing into his books that could appear otherwise than edifying, or at least morally un-objectionable. Yet the custom of calling a spade a spade was very prevalent in the seventeenth century; and writers, with no evil intent, alluded to matters that it is not now customary to mention. I have therefore thought it advisable not to trans-late one or two words of the "Labyrinth," nor one somewhat longer passage. I have marked such omissions by asterisks. On the other hand, a few expressions that may now be thought coarse, though they did not appear so in the seventeenth century, have been retained. The "Labyrinth" contains a certain number of Latin words. I have retained these, as they are not difficult to under-stand, and are very characteristic of Komensky's manner of writing. On the other hand, I have translated into English his Latin dedication of his book to Charles of Zerotin.

If this translation contributes, even to a slight degree, to making Komensky's masterpiece better known to English readers, I shall not think that the not inconsiderable labour that it involved has been in vain.

LÜTZOW.

ZAMPACH, *December 10, 1900.*

DEDICATION

To the Illustrious and truly noble Lord, LORD CHARLES,
BARON OF ZEROTIN, the elder, Captain of the
Land of Moravia.[1]

My Most Gracious Lord,

I SHOULD not venture in this but too turbulent time, full of disquietude, to molest your Illustriousness, oh, most Illustrious Lord! by this short letter, far less by the dedication of a book, were it not that the book is of those that aim at strengthening our minds and tranquillising them in God. I will explain how the matter stands. As in this my retreat and my painful inactivity, separated as I am from the cares of my vocation, I yet neither may be nor wish to be idle, I began within the last months to reflect on the vanity of the world (which I had various opportunities of beholding in divers places). Thus then was this work,[2] which I offer to your Illustriousness, born under my hands. The first part depicts the follies and inanity of the world, showing how mainly and with great labour it busies itself with worthless things, and how all these things at last end wretchedly, either in laughter or in tears. The second part describes, partly as through a veil, partly and openly the true and firm felicity

---

[1] In Latin "Pro-Marchio." The representative of the sovereign, called in German "Landeshauptmann," in Bohemian "Zemsky hejtman," presided at the meetings of the Moravian Diet. Zerotin held this office for some years.

[2] Komensky writes "drama."

of the sons of God ; for they are indeed happy who, turning
their backs on the world and all worldly things, adhere, and
indeed inhere, to God. I admit that what I offer here is but
begun, not completed. I see, indeed, that the subject is
very abundant, and so fit for sharpening the mind and re-
fining the style that it might, by the means of repeated new
conceptions, be enlarged almost to infinitude. Yet such as
the book is, I wish to collect its contents from my stray
papers and to offer it to your Illustriousness, for what purpose I dare not now clearly to say. But the sagacity of the
mind of your Illustriousness will perceive it while reading
the book, or will be able otherwise to explain it. This only
will I intimate, that I did not consider it inappropriate to offer
this work to one who, after having a thousand times experienced the storms and sorrows of the sea of the world,
has found repose in the most tranquil harbour of his conscience. Now it only remains to me to wish that your
Illustriousness, safe from the world and Satan, should live
gladly for Christ, and should joyfully and rightfully look forward to the future life that follows this one (alas, but a
wretched one !). Meanwhile, may the blessed spirit of God
our eternal Redeemer rule us, cheer us, console us, strengthen
us. Amen.

Written under the hill of Klopota, on the Ides of
December, 1623.

Of your Illustriousness,

The most Devoted Client,

J. A. COMENIUS.

TO THE READER

EVERY being, even an irrational one, tends to delighting in pleasant and useful things, and to desiring them. Therefore this is naturally particularly the case as regards man, in whom the innate reasoning power has developed that desire for the good and useful; and, indeed, it not only develops it, but induces a man to find more pleasure in a thing the more good, useful, and pleasant it is, and the more heartily to strive for it. Therefore the question arose long ago among learned men, where and in what that summit of good (*summum bonum*) is to be found at which the wishes of man could stop; that is to say, that point which a man having attained it in his mind could and should stop, having no longer anything further to wish for.

2. If, then, we notice this fact, we shall find not only that philosophers gave, and give, careful consideration to this question, and to the way in which it can be solved, but also generally that every man's mind endeavours to discover where and by what means he can obtain the greatest delight; and we find that almost all men, fleeing outward from themselves, seek in the world and its things wherewith to calm and quiet their minds; one by estates and riches, another by pleasure and sensuality,

another by glory and honours; another, again, by wisdom and learning, another by gay companionships, and so forth; generally all strive for outward things.

3. But that that cannot be found there, of that the wisest of men, Solomon, is witness; he who also sought solace for his mind, and who, having traversed and viewed the whole world, at last said: "I hate this life; because the work that is wrought under this sun is grievous unto me; for all is vanity and vexation of spirit."[1] When he had searched afterwards for the true solace of the spirit, he declared that it consists in this: that man, renouncing the world such as it is, should seek only our Lord God, fear Him, and heed His commandments. For this, he said, is the whole duty of man. Similarly, David found that that man is happiest who, dismissing the world from his eyes and his mind, trusts in the Lord God alone, considers Him his portion for ever, and dwells with Him in his heart.[2]

4. The mercy of God be praised that has opened my eyes also, so that I have learnt to recognise the manifold vanities of this world, and its miserable deceit that is hidden under its outer splendour; and also (have I learnt) to seek elsewhere the peace and security of my mind. Wishing suitably to place all this before mine own eyes, and also to show it to others, I have imagined this pilgrimage or wandering through the world; what monstrous

[1] Eccles. ii. 17.
[2] Psalm vii. 3.

things I have seen or met with, and where and how
I at last discovered the solace which I had vainly
sought in the world; all this I have, as it were,
depicted in this treatise. With how much wit, I
heed not. May God only grant that my work be
useful to myself and to my fellow-men!

5. It is not a poem,[1] reader, that you will read,
although it may have the seeming of a poem. It
contains true matter; understanding me, you will
easily recognise this; he, in particular, who has
some knowledge of my life and its incidents. For
I have mainly depicted the adventures that I have
already encountered in the not numerous years of
my life, though I have also described some incidents that I have seen in others, and things concerning them, of which information was given unto
me. I have not, however, alluded to all the
happenings that befell me, partly from bashfulness,
partly because I did not know what instruction
such a narrative would confer on others.

6. My guides, and indeed those of everyone
who gropes through this world, are two. *Insolence*
of the mind, which inquires into everything, and
inveterate custom with regard to all things, which
gives the colour of truth to the deceits of the world.
He who follows them prudently will, together with
me, recognise the wretched turmoil of his race; but
if it appears otherwise to him, let him know that

---

[1] The "Labyrinth" is neither rhymed nor written in blank
verse. Komensky uses the word "basen" (poem) rather in its
original signification of creation or fiction, in distinction from
an account of actual occurrences.

the spectacles of the general deception oppress his nose.

7. As regards the happy ways of those hearts that are devoted to God, this is described rather "in idea,"[1] and I do not wish to infer that all this befalls all those that are chosen. But God will have no lack of such chosen spirits, and every truly pious one will be bound to strive to reach the same degree of perfection. Farewell, dear Christian, and may the leader of light, the Holy Ghost, show thee better than I can both the vanity of the world and the glory, happiness, and pleasure of the chosen hearts that are united with God.

[1] *I.e.*, from my imagination.

THE LABYRINTH OF THE WORLD

CHAPTER I

ON THE CAUSES OF THIS MY PILGRIMAGE THROUGH THE WORLD

WHEN I had attained that age at which the difference between good and bad begins to appear to the human understanding, I saw how different are the ranks, conditions, occupations of men, the works and endeavours at which they toil ; and it seemed most necessary to me to consider what group of men I should join, and with what matters I should occupy my life.

(*The Fickleness of the Mind.*)

2. Thinking much and often on this matter, and weighing it diligently in my mind, I came to the decision that that fashion of life which contained least of cares and violence, and most comfort, peace, and cheerfulness pleased me most.

3. But then, again, it seemed to me difficult to know

which and what was my vocation, and I knew not of whom to seek counsel; nor did I greatly wish to consult anyone on this matter, thinking that each one would praise to me his own walk in life. Neither did I dare to grasp anything hastily, for I feared that I might not choose aright.

4. Yet, I confess, I secretly began to grasp first at one thing, then another, then a third, but each one I speedily abandoned, for I remarked (as it seemed to me) something of hardship and vanity in each. Meanwhile, I feared that my fickleness would bring me to shame. And I knew not what to do.

5. Thus yearning and turning the matter in solitude in my mind, I came to this decision that I should first behold all earthly things that are under the sun, and then only, having wisely compared one thing with another, choose a course of life, and obtain in some fashion the things necessary for leading a quiet life in the world. The more I thought the matter over, the more this matter pleased me.

CHAPTER II

THE PILGRIM OBTAINS IMPUDENCE AS A GUIDE

AND then I came out of my solitude—and began to look around, thinking how and whence to begin my voyage. At that very instant there appeared one coming, I knew not whence. His gait was active, his sight skilful, his speech quick, so that it seemed to me that his feet, his eyes, his tongue, all possessed great agility. He stepped up to me, and asked whence I came and whither I proposed to go? I said that I had left my home, and decided to wander through the world and obtain some experience.

(*The World a Labyrinth.*)

2. This pleased him well, and he said, "But where hast thou a guide?" I answered, "I have none. I trust to God and to my eyes, that they will not lead me astray." "Thou wilt not succeed," said he. "Hast thou heard of the labyrinth of Crete?" "I have heard somewhat," I answered. He then replied, "It was a wonder of the world, a building consisting of so many chambers, closets, and corridors, that he who entered it without a

guide walked and blundered through it in every direction, and never found the way out. But this was nothing compared to the way in which the labyrinth of this world is fashioned, particularly in these times. I do not, believe me, counsel a prudent man to enter it alone."

(Description of One who was insolent.)

3. "But where, then, shall I seek such a guide?" I asked. He answered: "I am able to guide those who wish to see and learn somewhat, and to show them where everything is; therefore, indeed, did I come to meet thee." Wondering, I said: "Who art thou, my friend?" He answered: "My name is Searchall, and I have the by-name of Impudence. I wander through the whole world, peep into all corners, inquire about the words and deeds of all men, see everything that is visible, spy out and discover everything that is secret; generally, nothing can befall without me. It is my duty to survey everything; and if thou comest with me, I shall lead thee to many secret places, whereto thou wouldst never have found thy way."

4. Hearing such speech, I begin to rejoice in my mind at having found such a guide, and beg him not to shun the labour of conducting me through the world. He answered: "As I have gladly served others in this matter, so will I gladly aid you also." And seizing my hand, "Let us go," he said, and we went; and I said: "Well, now will I gladly see what the ways of the world are, and

also whether it contains that on which a man may safely rely." Hearing this, my companion stopped and said : "Friend, if thou art starting on this voyage with the purpose, not of seeing our things with pleasure, but of passing judgment on them according to thine own understanding, I do not know if Her Majesty our Queen will be pleased with this."

(*Vanity, the Queen of the World.*)

5. "And who, then, is your Queen?" I said. He answered : "She who directs the whole world and its ways from the beginning. She is called Wisdom, though some wiseacres call her Vanity. I therefore warn thee in time, when we shall go there and look round, do not cavil; then wouldst thou draw some evil upon thyself, even though I be close to thee."

CHAPTER III

FALSEHOOD JOINS THEM

THUS, whilst he talks with me, behold someone steals up to us, a man or a woman (for he was wondrously muffled up, and something that seemed like mist surrounded him). "Impudence," he said, "whither dost thou hurry with this man?" "I am leading him into the world," he replied. "He wishes to behold it."

2. "And why without me?" the other again said. "Thou knowest that it is thy duty to conduct the pilgrims, mine to show them where things are. For it is not the wish of Her Majesty the Queen that anyone who enters her kingdom should himself interpret what he hears and sees according to his pleasure, or cavil too much. Rather doth she wish that all things that exist and their purposes be told him, and that he should content himself with that."

Impudence answered: "As if anyone could be so insolent as not to remain with the others; but this one, meseems, will require a bit." "It is well; let us go forward." Then he joined us, and we went on.

(*The Ways of Falsehood in the World.*)

3. I, however, thought in my mind: "Would God that I had not been led here! These are deliberating about some bit for my mouth." And I say to this, my new companion: "Friend, take it not amiss; gladly would I know thy name also." He answered: "I am the interpreter of Wisdom, the queen of the world, and I have the duty to teach all how they can understand the things of the world. Therefore I place in the minds of all, old and young, noble and of mean birth, ignorant and learned, all that belongs to true, worldly wisdom, and I lead them to joy and merriment, for without me even kings, princes, and the proudest men would be in strange anxiety, and would spend their time on earth mournfully."

4. On this I said: "Fortunately has God granted me thee as a guide, dear friend, if this is true. For I have set out for the world for the purpose of seeking what is safest and most gratifying in it, and then relying on it. Having now in thee so trusty a councillor, I shall easily be able to choose well." "Do not doubt this," he said, "for though in our kingdom thou wilt find everything most finely ordered and most gay, yet is it ever true that some professions and trades have more convenience and freedom than others. Thou wilt be able to choose from everything that which thou wishest. I will explain to thee everything as it is." I said: "By what name do men call thee?" He answered: "My name is Falsehood."

E

CHAPTER IV

THE PILGRIM RECEIVES A BRIDLE AND SPECTACLES

HEARING this, I was terrified, and thought within myself: "Alas, for my sins have I obtained such companions! That first one (thus my mind devised) spoke of some sort of bridle; the other one is called Falsehood. His queen he calls Vanity (though I think he imprudently blabbed this out); but what is this?"

2. And whilst I thus continue silently and with downcast eyes, and my feet move on somewhat reluctantly, Searchall says: "What, thou fickle one; methinks thou wishest to go back!" And before I could answer he threw a bridle over my neck, and suddenly a bit slipped into my mouth. "Now wilt thou," he said, "go obediently to the spot for which thou hast started?"

(*The Bridle of Vanity.*)

3. And I look at this bridle, and behold it was stitched together out of straps of pertness, and the bit was made out of the iron of obstinacy; and I understood that I should now no longer behold the world freely as before, but that I should be drawn

on forcibly by the inconstancy and disconsolateness of my mind.

(*The Spectacles of Falsehood.*)

4. Then my companion on the other side said: "And I give thee these spectacles, through which thou wilt henceforth look on the world," and he thrust on my nose spectacles, through which I immediately see everything differently than before. They certainly had this power (as I afterwards often experienced), that to him who saw through them distant things appeared near, near things distant; small things large, and large things small; ugly things beautiful, and beautiful things ugly; the white black, and the black white, and so forth. And I well understood that he should be called Falsehood who knew how to fashion such spectacles and place them on men.

(*The Spectacles are made of Illusion and Custom.*)

5. Now these spectacles, as I afterwards understood, were fashioned out of the glass of Illusion, and the rims which they were set in were of that horn which is named Custom.

6. But, fortunately for me, he had put them on me somewhat crookedly, so that they did not press closely on my eyes, and by raising my head and gazing upward I was still able clearly to see things in their natural way. I rejoiced over this, and said within myself: "Though you have closed my

mouth and covered my eyes, yet I trust in my God that you will not take from me my mind and my reason. I will go on, and I wonder what then this world is which the Lady Vanity wishes us to see, but not to see with our own eyes."

CHAPTER V

THE PILGRIM VIEWS THE WORLD FROM ON HIGH

(*There is Nothing beyond the World.*)

WHILE I am thus reflecting, behold, we find ourselves (I know not how) on a very high tower, and it seemed to me that I was immediately under the clouds. Gazing down from here, I see on the earth a town seemingly fine and beautiful, and very broad, but I could in every direction perceive its boundaries and limits. And it was built in the shape of a circle, and provided with walls and ramparts; and instead of a ditch there was a dark, deep valley, which, as it seemed to me, had neither banks nor bottom. For only above the city was there light; everywhere around it there was sheer darkness.

(*The Situation of the World.*)

2. Now I saw that the city itself was divided into countless streets, squares, houses, bigger and smaller buildings; and it was crowded with people as if with insects. To the east I saw a kind of gateway, from which a narrow street led to another gate that looked westward. From

the second gate only one entered into the various
streets of the city. I counted six principal streets
all running from east to west side by side, and in
the centre of them there was a large, round square
or market-place; behind it there stood to the west,
on a rocky, abrupt hillock, a high and splendid
castle, at which almost all the inhabitants of the
town gazed.

(*The Gate of Entrance and the Gate of Separation.*)

3. And my guide, Impudence, said to me: "Here,
pilgrim, thou hast this dear world which thou wast
so desirous to behold. I have, therefore, first led
thee to this height that thou mayest gaze on the
whole world, and understand its order.. That
eastern gate is the gate of life, through which all
pass who come to live in the world. That second
gate is the gate of separation, whence each person,
according to the lot he draws, betakes himself to
this or that calling.

(*The Conditions of Life are divided into Six Orders.*)

4. "The streets, then, which thou beholdest are
the various estates, orders, and avocations which
men choose. Thou seest six principal streets. In
this one to the south those who belong to the state
of domestic life reside—parents, children, and servants. In the next street live the tradesmen and
all who are busied in commerce. In that third
street, which is nearest the market-place, live the

learned men, who are employed on the works of the mind. On the other side, again, is the order of the clergy, by means of whom others avoid practising religion. Behind them is the order of the magistrates and rulers of the world. At last, to the north, we find the order of knighthood, which is employed in all the arts of war. And oh, how noble this is! These beget all; these feed all; these teach all; these pray for all; these judge all and preserve them from disorders; these fight for all; and all these serve each other, and all have equal rights.

(*The Castle of Fortune. The Market-place and the Castle of the World.*)

5. " Then that castle to the west is Arx Fortunæ, the castle of Fortune, in which chosen people live, who there enjoy riches, pleasure, and glory. The central market-place is for all ; for here men of all classes meet, and discuss what is necessary. In the middle of the market-place is, as it were, the centre of everything—that is the residence of Wisdom, the queen of the world."

(*The Beginning of the Confusion.*)

6. And this good order pleased me, and I began to praise God that He had so nobly divided the estates of men. But what pleased me not was that I saw that these streets were broken through in many places, so that sometimes one ran into another,

and this seemed to me a token that confusion and error might easily happen. Also when I looked at the roundness of the globe, I clearly saw that it moved and turned as in a circle, so that I feared lest I should become giddy. For when I cast my eyes here and there, I saw that in every direction everything swarmed with men. When I inclined my ears, everything was full of knocking, stamping, scrubbing, whispering, and screaming.

(*There was Deceit also.*)

7. And my interpreter, Falsehood, said: "Thou seest, dear friend, how delightful this world is, and how everything in it is noble; and that, even when thou viewest it from afar. What, then, wilt thou say later when thou beholdest it clearly with its delight. And to whom would it not be pleasant to be in the world?" I said, "Viewed from a distance, it pleases me; I know not how it will be later." "Well, in every way," he said; "only trust me, and we will go hence."

(*The Fashion of the Life of Childhood.*)

Impudence said: "Wait, I will also show him that spot to which we shall not come afterwards. Look, then, backwards towards sunrise; dost thou not see that something crawleth through that dark gate and creepeth towards us?" "I see it," I said. And he again: "These are people who—whence they themselves know not—have newly arrived in the world; neither do they as yet know that they are human beings; therefore darkness is around them, and naught but moaning and crying. But while they go along this street, grey light and dawn slowly come to them, till they come to that gate beneath us.   Let us go on and see what is doing there."

CHAPTER VI

FATE DISTRIBUTES VOCATIONS

(*Fate, the Gate of Life.*)

AND we go downward by a dark winding
staircase, and behold, before the door there was a
wide hall full of young folk, and on the right side
there sat a fierce-looking, old man,[1] who in his hand
held a large copper urn, and I saw that all those
who came through the gate of life stepped up to
him, and each one put his hand into the urn and
drew from it a tablet on which something was
written. Then each one of them went down one
of the streets, some running and shouting for joy,
while others crept along slowly, looked around
them, groaned and lamented.

(*The Callings are distributed.*)

2. And I step near and looked at the tablets
of some of them, and I see that one had drawn the

---

[1] " Ad eandem portam vir quidam senex astabat, aliquid
quasi innuens virorum turbae nobis haud intelligentibus quid
id esset. . . . Hic autem senex quem stantem videtis et
habentem altera manu chartam . . . is angelus est qui
præcepta dat ei qui tendit ad hunc mundum. . . . Et
etiam ostendit viam quam si sucedat salvus in ea evadit."—
"Tabula Cebetis," Edition of Leyden, 1640.

word: Rule! another: Serve! another: Command! another: Obey! another: Write! another: Plough! yet another: Learn! another: Dig! another: Judge! another: Fight! and so forth. Impudence says to me: "Here vocations and work are distributed, and according to this distribution each one has to fulfil his task in the world. He, however, who apportions the lots is called Fate, and from him must everyone who enters the world receive his instructions."

(*The Pilgrim begs first to be allowed to behold Everything.*)

3. Meanwhile, Falsehood nudged me at the other side, thus indicating that I also should stretch forth my hand. I begged not to be obliged to choose any one lot directly without first examining it, and entrust myself blindly to fortune. But I was told that without the knowledge and the permission of the lord regent, Fate, this could not be. Then stepping up to him, I modestly brought forward my request, saying that I had arrived with the intention of seeing everything for myself, and then only choosing what pleased me.

(*The Pilgrim receives the Permission.*)

He answered: "Oh, son, thou seest that others do not thus; what is given or offered them

they take.   However, as thou desirest this, it is
well."   Then he wrote on a scrap of paper: " Specu-
lare " (that is, " look around you," or "inquire"), gave
it me, and left me.

CHAPTER VII

THE PILGRIM BEHOLDS THE MARKET-PLACE OF THE WORLD

(*He sees the Diversity of Men.*)

AND my guide says to me: "As thou hast to see everything, let us first go to the market-place." And he leads me forth. And behold I see countless multitudes as a mist. For there were there people from the whole world, of every language and nation, of every age, growth, sex, estate, class, and profession. When first gazing at them, I see how strangely they sway to and fro, like the swarming of bees, and, indeed, far more wondrous.

(*The Various Characters and Gestures of Men.*)

2. For some walked, some ran, some rode, some stood, some sat, some rose up, some again reclined, some turned in various directions; some were alone, others in larger or smaller troops. Their dress and appearance varied much; some were stark naked, and had wondrous gestures. When some met one another there was various juggling with hands, mouth, knees, and otherwise; saluting and bowing,

77

and other foolish ways. And my guide says to me :
" Here hast thou that noble human race, that delightful creation, which has been granted sense and
immortality. How it bears on it the image of the
infinite God, and the likeness to Him, that wilt
thou recognise by the variety of His creations. As
in a looking-glass wilt thou see the worth of this
thy human race."

(*Hypocrisy in All.*)

3. I then look at them more carefully, and see
directly that everyone in the crowd, when walking
among the others, wore a mask on his face ; but on
going away, when he was alone, or among his
equals, he pulled it off, and when he had to go
among the throng, he again fastened it on. And
I ask what this means. The guide answered :
" That, my dear son, is worldly prudence, so that
each man may not show to all what he is. Alone
in his home a man may be as he is, but before
others it is beseeming that he appear affable, and
that he assume a mien." Then the desire befell me
more carefully to watch how these people might be
without this dissembling covering.

(*Their Wondrous Deformities.*)

4. And looking attentively at this, I see that
both in their face and in their bodies all are in
various ways deformed. Almost all were pimpled,
mangy, or leprous ; and besides, this one had a

pig's lip, another teeth as a dog, another the horns
of an ox, another donkey's ears, another eyes of a
basilisk, another the brush of a fox, another the
claws of a wolf. Some did I see with a peacock's
neck stretched out on high; others with the bristling
crest of a lapwing; others with horses' hoofs, and
so forth; mostly, however, they had the similitude
of apes.[1] And I am frightened, and say: "Nay,
here, meseems, I see monsters!" "What, froward
one" (the guide said), "thou speakest of monsters,"
and he threatened me with his fist. "Look but well
through thy spectacles, and thou wilt see that they
are men." But some of those who were passing
heard that I had called them monsters, stood still
and growled at me, and even threatened me, as if
they would attack me. Then having understood that
to reason here was vain, I became silent, and
thought within myself: "If they will be human
beings, let them be so; but as for me, what I see, I
see." I then feared that my guide would press
down my spectacles more firmly and mislead me;
therefore did I decide to be silent, and rather quietly
to behold these fine things of which I had seen the
beginning. I then gaze again, and I see how art-
fully some handled these masks, quickly removing
them and then again putting them on, so that they
were able to give themselves a different mien, whenever they saw that this was to their advantage.

---

[1] Compare with this : " At bottom they are all respectable,
pompous horse-faces, and self-opinionated donkey-muzzles,
and lop-eared, low-browed dog-sculls, and fatted swine-snouts,
and sometimes dull, brutal bull-fronts as well."—Ibsen,
" When we Dead awaken."

And then I already began somewhat to understand the course of the world, but I was silent.

(*General Misunderstanding among all Men.*)

5. I also observe and hear that they talked among themselves in various languages, so that they mostly did not understand or answer each other, or they answered on something different from what had been said, each one differently. Wherever a large crowd gathered, almost all spoke, each one listening to himself and none to the others, although they plucked at one another to attract attention. But it happened not thus; rather was there brawling and scuffling. And I exclaim: "In the name of God, are we then in Babel? Here each one sings his own song.[1] Could there be greater confusion?"

(*They occupy Themselves with Useless Matters.*)

6. Hardly anyone there was idle; all were employed in some kind of work; but these works —and this I never should have believed—were nothing but childish games, and at least were useless exertion. Some, indeed, collected sweepings and divided them amongst themselves; some hurried here and there with timber and stones, or dragged them up with a windlass, and then again dropped them; some dug up earth, and conveyed or carried it from place to place; the others

[1] A proverbial expression in Bohemian.

occupied themselves with little bells, looking-glasses, alembics, rattles, and other playthings; others also played with their own shadow, measuring, and pursuing it, and catching at it; and all this so vigorously that many groaned and sweated, and some, indeed, also injured themselves. And almost everywhere there were certain officers who ordered and measured out these labours with great heartiness, and with no less heartiness the others obeyed them. Wondering, I said, "Alas! Oh, wherefore does man exist, if he employs the sharpness of his heavenly talents for such vain and evil endeavours?" "Why vain?" said the interpreter. "Cannot one then see here, as in a looking-glass, how men accomplish everything by means of their talents? One does this, another that." "But all," I said, "work at such useless things, which are not adequate to their glorious eminence." "Do not cavil too much," he again said. "They are not yet in heaven, and in the world they must employ themselves with worldly matters. Thou wilt see in how orderly a fashion everything is done among them."

(*Fearful Disorder.*)

7. Then looking again, I see that nothing more disorderly could have been imagined; for when one laboured at a thing, and exerted himself, another, approaching him, meddled with the matter; thence quarrels, scuffles, fights. Then they reconciled themselves, and after a while fought again.

F

Sometimes several laid hold of one thing; then again they all left it, and ran off in different directions. Those, indeed, who were under the power of the officers and inspectors more or less kept to that which was appointed to them, for they were forced to do so. Yet here also I saw much confusion. Some broke away from their appointed places, and ran away; others contradicted the overseers, being unwilling to do what was ordered them; others attacked them with cudgels and robbed; indeed, everything, was disorderly. But as all this had to be called order, I dared not say anything.

(Everything full of Scandal and Evil Example.)

8. I also perceived other disorder, blindness, and folly. The whole of this market-place was—as were also the streets afterwards—full of holes, pits, and ravines, also of timber and stones, that lay about in every direction, and of other things. No one, however, put anything away, repaired it, or put it in proper order. On the contrary, they walked on unawares, so that first one, then another, knocked against something, fell, and either was killed or knocked down, and my heart quivered, beholding this. But among them, none took notice of this; indeed, when anyone fell they laughed at him. Then seeing a stalk, or the trunk of a tree, or a hole over which some blindly blundered, I began to caution them, but nobody heeded. Some laughed at me, others reviled me, others wanted to

beat me. Some fell and did not rise again; others rose again, and then again fell head over heels on the top of one another. Of weals and bruises everyone had enough, but they nowise heeded them, so that I could not but wonder at this their dulness, which counted their own falls and wounds for so little; while when one offended another, that one immediately rose in arms and warred with him.

(The Fickleness and Unsteadiness of Mankind in all Matters.)

9. I also perceived among men great delight in novelties and changes with regard to clothing, building, speech, gait, and other matters. Some, I saw, who did nothing but change their attire, wearing sometimes this, sometimes that manner of clothing; others imagined a new fashion of building, and after a while destroyed it again. While working they seized now this thing, now that, and then again abandoned it, seemingly through inconstancy. For if one died because of the burden under which he laboured or if he abandoned it, then immediately others were found who disputed it, squabbled and fought about it in a wondrous fashion. Among them all there was none who spoke, or did something, or erected an edifice, without the others laughing at it, misrepresenting it, destroying it. One fashioned a thing with vast labour and expense, finding in it great pleasure, then another, approaching him, overturned, de-

stroyed, and injured it, so that I saw that never in the world a man made a thing without another injuring it. Some, indeed, did not wait for others; they themselves destroyed their own works, so that I wondered at their fickleness and their vain endeavours.

(*Their Pride and Presumption.*)

10. I also saw that many walked on high pattens; others made themselves stilts (so that, raised above all, they could view everything from above), and thus did they strut about. But the higher one was the more easily was he upset, or others (from jealousy, I presume), tripped up his feet; this happened to many, and they drew the laughter of all on them. Of such instances saw I many.

(*Death, which miserably destroyeth All.*)

11. At last I saw Death stalking about everywhere among them, and she was provided with a sharp scythe, and with a bow and arrows, and with a loud voice she exhorted all to remember that they were mortal; but none listened to her call. Each one was none the less intent on his folly and his misdeeds. Then seizing these arrows, she threw them at the people in every direction, and struck down this or that one from among them, young or old, poor or rich, learned or unlearned, without distinction, so that they fell down. He who was

struck down screamed, shrieked, and roared ; those who were walking near ran a little farther off, and soon again took no notice.   Some coming near gazed at the wounded man, who was rattling in the throat, and when he contracted his feet and ceased breathing, they called each other together, sang round him, ate, drank, and shouted,[1] and some somewhat mocked at this.   Then they seized the dead man and threw him over the boundaries into that gloomy pit which surrounds the world, and returning thence they again revelled ; but none escaped Death, though they diligently endeavoured not to heed her, even when she closely brushed against them.

(*Various Diseases.*)

12. I then saw that not all whom she (Death) struck fell dead to the ground ; some she merely wounded, lamed, blinded, deafened, or stunned. Some after their wound swelled out like a blister, others dried up as a splinter, others trembled like an aspen-leaf, and so forth.   Thus did a larger number of men walk to and fro wounded, and with rotting and soured limbs, than there were healthy people.

(*Help against this is vainly sought.*)

13. And I saw many running to and fro who sold plasters, ointments, waters, as remedies for

---

[1] It is perhaps scarcely necessary to mention that Komensky here alludes sarcastically to the feasting at funerals that was particularly prevalent in his time.

these wounds. And all bought these things from them, exulting thereon and defying Death. But she heeded not, and indeed struck down and overthrew even these venders themselves. And it was a mournful spectacle for me to behold how pitiably, how suddenly, and by what manifold deaths a creature destined to immortality perisheth. I also found, in particular, that when one was most ready for life, gathered his friends together, made plans for his future life, built houses, scraped money together, and otherwise strove for his own welfare, then the arrow of Death struck him and made an end to everything, and he who had prepared for himself a dwelling in the world was very often torn away from it and his goods became useless; then another succeeded him, and the same fate befell him, and so equally the third, the tenth, the hundredth. But when I saw that none would understand the uncertainty of life, and take it to heart—indeed, that though standing close to the abyss of death they behaved as if they were certain of immortality (and it is marvellous that my heart did not burst from grief)—then I desired to raise my voice to exhort and beg them to open their eyes, and to behold Death preparing her arrows, and in some fashion to strive to escape them. But I understood that as Death herself could, by her constant cries and her incessant appearance before them in her terrible shape, achieve nothing, my feeble speech would indeed be fruitless. I then said in a low voice: " It is for ever pitiful before God that we miserable mortals should for our misfortune be so blind." The interpreter answered me: " My good man, would it then be wisdom to torment ourselves by think-ing of death? Just because everyone knows he cannot escape her, it is better not to heed her, but to look at one's own goods, and to be of a cheerful mind. If she comes, she comes. In some hours everything will be at an end, and perhaps even in an instant. Why, therefore, should, because some die, the others cease to be merry? For in the place of each one how many again are born." To this I said: " If wisdom consists in this, then I understand it amiss," and then I was silent.

(Men are themselves the Causes of their Diseases and Death.)

14. But I will not conceal this, that when I beheld the countless number of Death's arrows, it came into my mind: " Whence, then, does Death take that mass of arrows, that she never exhausts them ? " And I look, and behold quite clearly that she had no arrows at all, but only a bow; the arrows she took from the people, each one from that person whom she intended to strike. And I observed that these people themselves trimmed and prepared these arrows, some even pertly and audaciously carried them to her, so that it was sufficient for her to take the arrows from them and to shoot them in the heart. And I cried: " Now I see that it is true: 'Et mortis faber est quilibet ipse suæ.' " I already see that no one dies who

had not by his greediness, intemperance, frowardness, lastly by his indiscretion, brought on himself
abscesses, boils, outer or inner wounds (for these
are the arrows of Death).   But while I thus carefully gaze on Death, and the way she seized the
people, Falsehood pulls me away and says:
" Wherefore, foolish one, dost thou look rather at
the dead than at the living ?   When one dies, then
it is over with him ; but strive thou to live ! "

CHAPTER VIII

THE PILGRIM BEHOLDS THE STATE OF MATRIMONY

(*The Preparation to this State is toilsome and anxious.*)

AND they lead me forward, and bring me to a
street where, they said, married people lived, and
they said also that the fashion of this delightful
life would be pleasing unto me. And behold, there
was a gate which, as they said, was called Betrothment; in front of it there was a wide square,
in which crowds of people of both sexes walked
about, and each one looked into the eyes of the
other; and not only this, but they also looked at
one another's ears, nose, teeth, neck, tongue, hands,
feet, and other limbs; also did each measure the
other—how tall, how broad, how stout, or how
slender he was. Then one approached another,
and then again stepped apart from him, examining him now in front, now from the back, now
from the right side, now from the left, and
observing everything that he beheld of him.
Each one particularly examined (and this I saw
most frequently) the bags, purses, and pouches of
the other, measuring and weighing how long, how
broad, how full, how heavy, or how light they

were. Sometimes several men pointed to one
woman, and then none took her. One man drove
another away, and they quarrelled, struggled, and
fought; murders also did I here behold. Then
one man pushed another away, and was himself
again pushed away; some, after driving others
away, then ran away themselves. Yet another
man, not lingering to examine, seized her who
was nearest, and the couple lead each other hand-
in-hand through the gate. Seeing much fooling
of this fashion, I asked: "What, then, are these
people doing?" The interpreter answered: "They
are those who would gladly enter the street of
Matrimony; but as no one is allowed to pass
through yonder gate alone, but only in pairs, each
one must choose himself a companion. Therefore
is this choosing done here, and everyone seeks
what is convenient to him; he who finds it goes,
as you see, to the gate with his companion."
"And could not this choosing be done in a somewhat easier fashion?" I said. "How mightily
toilsome this is!" He answered: "This is not
labour, but pleasure. Dost thou not see how
merrily they bear themselves; how they laugh,
how they exult. No fashion of life, believe me,
is merrier than this one." Then I look, and see
that some indeed laughed and exulted; but I see
others also who hang down their heads dolefully,
turn round, drag each other backwards and for-
wards, then again retreat; they grieve, do not
sleep or eat, and even become mad. And I say:
"What of these?" He answered: "This also is

pleasure." "Be it so," I said; "let us proceed and see what befalls farther on."

(Great Uncertainty as to how they should sit together.)

2. Then forcing our way through the crowd, we arrive at the gate itself; and lo! before we entered it, we behold a balance suspended, which was provided with two baskets as scales, and round it stood the crowd. And they placed each of these couples in the baskets opposite one another, and watched whether the balance was even; and in various fashions they descended, then separated, shook the scales, and then again steadied them. Then only when they had sufficiently weighed them they allowed them to pass through the gate. But not all fared equally well. For some fell through the basket, were derided, and had to troop away with shame, and took themselves off; they even crammed a hood or sack over the ears of some, and made merry at their expense. And seeing this, I asked: "What, then, is done here?" The answer was: "This is done that the betrothment may be safe; for if the scales show that they are even and equal, they are, as you see, allowed to enter this state of matrimony; if it is otherwise, they separate." "And what, then, do they here consider as equality?" I said, "for indeed I see that the balance proves some to be equal in age, estate, and in every fashion, and yet they allow one of the two to

fall through the basket. Others, on the other hand, who are most unequal they place together— old men and young girls, young men and old women. One stands upright, and the other bends downward, and yet they say that they may be joined; how is this?" He answered: "Thou dost not see everything. It is true that some old man or old woman may not be worth a pound of tow,[1] yet if they have either a fat pouch or a hat before which other hats are lowered, or something similar (for all these things are weighed in the scales), the matter does not stand as it appears to your judgment."

(The Fashion in which they sit together is unalterable.)

3. Entering after those whom they allowed to pass, I see at the gate men who seemed smiths; these clasp on each couple awful fetters, and only when fettered allow them to pass. Many people were present at this fettering who (as they said) were invited for the purpose of being witnesses. These played and sang before them, and bade them be of good cheer. But watching carefully, I remarked that they did not fasten up these fetters with a padlock as with other prisoners, but that they immediately forged, welded, soldered them together, so that, as long as their lives in this world lasted, they could not unbuckle them or tear them off. This frightened me, and I said: "Oh, most cruel captivity! if anyone once enters it, for all

[1] A proverbial expression in Bohemia.

eternity he has no hope of recovering his liberty."
The interpreter answered : " Certainly this of all
human bonds is the most rigid ; but the sweetness
of this state is such that man gladly passes under
the yoke ; thou wilt see for thyself what a delightful
life it is." " Let us then go among them, that I
may see," I said.

*(There is little Pleasure even when Marriage is most
successful.)*

4. We then enter the street, and behold, there
was a host of people all in couples, but many, as it
seemed to me, most unequally joined, big ones with
small ones, handsome ones with ugly ones, young
ones with old ones, and so forth. And examining
carefully what they were doing, and in what the
sweetness of this state consisted, I see that they
look at each other, speak to one another, and sometimes one caressed and also kissed the other. " Here
you see," said the interpreter to me, " what a pure
thing wedlock is, when it is successful." " Then
this," said I, " is the summa of all ? " " Certainly,"
he said. And I again, " Then there is indeed but
little pleasure ; and whether it is worth such fetters,
I know not."

*(The Misery and Worry of all Married
People generally.)*

5. I now look further about me among them,
and witness how much toil and anxiety the

wretched people had. They mostly had children
around them, who were attached to them by
bridles ; these screamed, squalled, stank, soiled
themselves, groaned, and died, and I am silent as
regards the pain, the tears, the dangers to the
lives of their mothers, with which they entered
into the world. If a child grew up there was
twofold trouble with it; one was to hold it back by
means of the bridle, the other to drive it on by
means of *the* spur; and often the children, suffering
neither bridle nor spur, made wondrous mis-
chievous endeavours, causing to their parents
weariness and tears. But if they allowed them to
act according to their will or tore themselves away
from them, shame and death herethrough befell
the parents. And marking this, I began to admonish some of the people, both parents and
children, warning the former against foolish
love for their children and too great forbearance
with them, whilst I admonished the latter to be
somewhat more virtuous. But I achieved little
beyond this, that they looked at me peevishly,
threw jests at me, and some even menaced to kill
me. And when I saw some who were sterile I
declared them happy ; but they also complained
and lamented that their life was joyless. Thus,
then, did I understand that both to have and not
to have offspring is misery. Also had almost each
couple with them and around them stranger folk
to serve them and theirs ; they often had to bestow
more care on these than on themselves and their
family, and besides had to suffer much discomfort

through them. Also were there here, as in that
market-place, many implements and stumbling-
blocks, wood, stones, and pits ; when one stumbled,
he tripped up the other also, fell and injured the
other also ; the other, unable to leave him, had
equally with him to whimper, cry, and suffer pain.
Thus did I understand that everyone in this state,
instead of one care, anxiety, danger, has to suffer
as many cares, anxieties, dangers as there are
people to whom he is tied. And this state pleased
me not.

(*The awful Tragedy of luckless Marriage.*)

6. While I was then gazing at some of these in
the crowd, I beheld a tragedy. Two were joined
together who were assuredly not of one will; one
wanted to go this way, the other that ; then they
quarrelled, disputed, wrangled. One complained
to the passers-by of this, the other of that ; and
then when there was nobody to arbitrate between
them, they attacked one another, and cuffed and
cudgelled each other in an ugly fashion. If some
one reconciled them, after a while they quarrelled
again. Some for a long time disputed in words
whether they should go to the right or to the left,
and as each obstinately insisted on what he wished,
one with all his might flung himself in the
direction he wished to go, and the other also in the
opposite direction. Then there was a struggle and
a mournful spectacle who would overcome the
other ; sometimes the man triumphed and dragged

the woman after him, although she caught at the ground, the grass, or whatever she could; sometimes the man had to follow the woman, and the others laughed at this. But this seemed to me a matter worthy rather of pity than of laughter; particularly when I saw that during this torment some shed tears, groaned, wrung their hands heavenward, declaring that they wished by means of gold and silver to redeem themselves from this bond. And I said to my interpreter: "Can no help, then, be granted them? Can they not be untied and set free from one another, they who cannot be reconciled?" "That cannot be," he said; "as long as they live they must continue thus." "Oh, this cruel bondage and slavery! This is indeed worse than death!" And he again: "Why, then, did they not previously reflect more wisely? They deserve their fate; let them continue in their dissensions."

(*Voluntary Slavery*.)

7. Then I gaze, and lo! Death, with her arrows, strikes down some and overthrows them, and immediately the fetters of each of them were loosened. And I wished them joy of this, thinking that they also would wish themselves joy, and be heartily glad of this relief. But behold, almost every one of them began to cry and lament in a fashion that hardly ever I had heard in the world, wringing their hands and complaining of their misfortunes. Of those whom I had before seen living peaceably together, I understood that one really

grieved for the death of the other. I thought, however, that they only dissembled thus before the people. I vowed that they would repent their error, and teach others to beware of these bonds. But these, before I had time to observe, wiped their eyes again, ran outside, and returned afresh in new fetters. And I said with wrath: "Oh, ye monsters! ye are unworthy of pity;" and to my guide: "Let us from hence; I find in this state more of vanity than anything else."

(The Pilgrim also receives Fetters.)

8. Meanwhile (for I must not be silent as regards my own adventures), while we are returning to the gate of separation, and though my intention is further to look on the world, my guides, both Impudence and Falsehood, begin strongly to urge me to try myself, also, the state of matrimony; thus would I better understand it. I replied that I was young, that the examples I had seen terrified me, that I had not yet beheld everything in the world, and so forth. But this availed not; they induced me to go on to the scales, as it were in sport, and then into bonds, and I proceeded as one of four who were joined together; they also added to our party a number of others (they said it was that they should be my servants, and for the sake of modesty); so that, gasping and groaning, I could hardly drag them along with me. Then suddenly a tempest came down, with lightning, thunder, and a terrible fall of hail; and all those around me

G

dispersed, except those who were joined to me. With these I hurry into a corner, but Death, with her arrows, strikes down my three companions, so that, mournfully solitary and stunned by horror, I knew not what to do. My guides said that this was a favourable moment, and that I could now easily flee. And I said: "Why, then, did you advise me to come here?" They answered that there was no time for disputing; rather should I flee. And thus did I hurry away.

(The Pilgrim's Judgment on the State of Matrimony.)

9. And having escaped thence, I yet do not know what I should say about this state, whether it affords more pleasure when it is successful (which I presume would have been the case with me), or more woe from various causes. That only I remember that both without it and within it there is much anxiety, and even when it is successful, the sweet is mixed with the bitter.

CHAPTER IX

THE PILGRIM EXAMINES THE ORDER OF THE TRADESMEN

(*What he saw there Publicly.*)

THEN walking on, we arrive in a street where trades were carried on ; this street was again divided into many smaller streets and squares, and everything was full of various halls, workshops, forges, working-rooms, shops, and booths, with various wondrous tools ; the people turned round them in a strange fashion, with much crashing, banging, piping, blowing, hulloaing, rattling, and scrubbing in various ways. I saw here that some scraped the earth and opened mines in it, either ripping it up on the surface or digging deep into its interior like moles. Others paddled in the water, on rivers, or on the sea ; others stirred fires ; others gaped at the air ; others busied themselves with wild beasts ; others with stones and wood ; others conveyed various goods to and fro. And the interpreter said to me : " See what ingenious and pleasant work this is ; well, what here pleases thee most ? " I said, " It may be that there is here somewhat of merriment ; but with it I see much toiling, I hear much moaning." " Not all labour is so arduous," he said : " let us look more closely into these various matters." And they led me turn by turn through these places, and I viewed everything, and for the sake of experience sometimes touched this thing or that; but I neither can nor will describe everything in this spot. Only what I saw openly that I will not conceal.

(*All Trades are Perilous Strivings.*)

Firstly, I saw that all these worldly traffics are but labour and vain striving, and that each has its discomfort and danger. I saw, indeed, that those who dealt with fire were sunburnt and sooty like Moors; the clattering of hammers ever hummed in their ears and half hindered their hearing; the gleam of the fires ever sparkled in their eyes, and their skins were blistered and cracked. Those who carried on their trade in the earth had darkness and horror for companions, and not rarely did it happen that they were buried in the earth. Those who worked on the waters became as moist as a thatched roof; like aspen leaves, they shivered from the cold, their bowels became raw,[1] and many of them became the prey of the deep. Those who busied themselves with wood, stones, and other materials were full of weals, groaning, and fatigue. I also saw how stupid were the labours of some, who yet toiled and strove till they sweated, became fatigued, fell down, injured themselves, overworked themselves; yet, with all their miserable exertion, they barely succeeded in obtaining their daily

---

[1] *I.e.,* their digestion became impaired.

bread. It is true that I saw others who lived more easily and more advantageously; but the less labour there was, the more was there of vice and fraud.

(*Incessant Striving.*)

Secondly, I saw that all the work of man is for his mouth; for whatever a man acquired that he stuffed into his own mouth, or into those of the members of his family; I must except the few who placed in their wallets that of which they deprived their mouth; but these wallets, I again saw, were full of holes; what was heaped into them streamed out again, and others gathered it up; sometimes one approached and tore the wallet away; or one stumbling against another plucked or tore away the wallet, or he lost it through some other mishap; thus did I see clearly that all these worldly employments are but as the pouring out of overflowing water; money is won and then again lost, with but this difference that it flees more easily than it approaches, whether it is absorbed by the mouth or by the money-chest. Therefore did I see more poor men than rich.

(*Hard Striving.*)

Thirdly, did I see that each of these labours required the entire strength of a man; if one did but look backward or somewhat tarry, he immediately remained behind; immediately everything dropped out of his hands, and before he was aware of it he was ruined.

(*Difficult Striving.*)

Fourthly, I beheld everywhere much hardship. Before a man was well prepared for his trade a good part of his life had passed, and even afterwards, unless he was constantly attentive, all his concerns again went backward; indeed, even among those who were the most attentive, as many, I found, met with loss than with gain.

(*Striving that kindles Jealousy.*)

Fifthly, did I behold among all (particularly among those of the same trade) much hatred and malice. If more work was carried to one, or more was brought forth from his shop, the neighbours immediately looked askance at him, gnashed their teeth at him, and, when able, spoilt his wares; thence arose dissensions, discord, cursing; and some, out of impatience, threw down their tools, and defying the others, gave themselves up to idleness and voluntary poverty.

(*Sinful Striving.*)

Sixthly, I beheld everywhere much deceit and fraud. Their work, particularly that done for others, was done hurriedly and carelessly; yet, meanwhile, they extolled and praised their work as much as they could.

(*Vain and Unnecessary Striving.*)

Seventhly, I found there[1] many unnecessary vanities, for I clearly understood that these occupations were mainly nothing but vanity and useless folly. For as the human body can certainly be sustained by little and very simple food and drink, as it can be clothed with few and very simple garments, and sheltered by a small and very simple building, therefore is it clear that but small and simple trouble and labour are required for these purposes, as *was* indeed the case in ancient times. This also I found here, that the world either will not or cannot judge rightly; for men have become accustomed to employ so many and such rare things for the purpose of filling their bellies with food and drink, that to obtain these things a large portion of the people have to work by land and on the sea, and to imperil their strength and their life; while others, again, have to be special masters in the art of preparing these things. Similarly, no small part of the people was employed in seeking various materials for clothing and building, and in giving them manifold monstrous shapes; all this is useless and vain, and often even sinful. Likewise did I see craftsmen whose whole art and labour consisted in making childish trifles, or other toys, for the

[1] *I.e.*, among the order of the tradesmen.

purpose of causing amusement and wasting time; others, again, there were whose work it was to prepare and to multiply the instruments of cruelty against mankind, such as swords, daggers, battle clubs, muskets, and so forth. With what conscience and what pleasure of mind men could attend to all these trades, I do not know. But this I know, that if all that was useless, unnecessary, and sinful had been taken away and eliminated, the larger part of men's trade would have had to sink to the ground. Therefore for this, and for the other reasons mentioned before, my mind could find pleasure in nothing here.

(Striving that beseemed Brutes rather than Men.)

This was particularly the case when I saw that men worked only with the body and for the body, though man possessing a superior thing, namely, the soul, should bestow most care on it, and seek principally its advantage.

9. One thing, meseems, I should specially relate, how I fared among the waggoners on land and among the sailors on the sea. When I was thus depressed while visiting the workshops of the handicraftsmen, Impudence said to Falsehood: "I see that this man is restless, and wishes to constantly move like quicksilver; therefore is there no place that pleaseth him, and to which he would desire to be attached. Let us show him the freer profession of the trades who are at liberty to transport themselves from one place in the world

to another, and fly about like birds." "I am not,"
I said, "contrary to seeing this also." Then we
went on.

(The Toilsome Life of Waggoners.)

10. And then I immediately see a crowd of men
who were turning round and round, and were
gathering, collecting, and lifting up various things,
even chips, morsels of earth and manure, and these
they bound together in bundles. "What is this?"
I ask. They said that these were preparing to
travel across the world. And I: "But why do they
not voyage without these burdens? They would
proceed more easily." The guides answered: "Thou
art a fool. How could they journey otherwise?
These things are their wings." "Wings?" say I.
"Certainly wings; for these give to them resolution
and courage, and also ensure to them freer passage
and safe course. Dost thou then think that men
are allowed to rove vainly through the world? In
this fashion must men obtain their livelihood,
favour, and everything else." I then gaze, and lo!
they heaped as many goods as they could find on
a thing that seemed a pedestal with underlying
wheels; this they rolled and screwed, and harnessed
cattle to it; they then with all these goods toiled
and plodded across hills, mountains, valleys and
ravines, rejoicing in their minds over their merry
life; and such it appeared to me also just at first.
But when I saw them sticking in the mire, soiling
themselves, puddling in the mud, labouring and

striving; also that from rain, snow, sleet, snow-drifts, cold, and heat they suffered much discomfort; and when I also saw that everywhere on the mountain passes men lay in ambush for them and emptied their pouches (and to escape this, neither wrath, nor scuffling, nor raging availed), and that on the highroads a rapacious rabble attacked them, then I lost all pleasure in this order.

(*The Discomfort of a Sailor's Life.*)

11. They then said that there was a more convenient fashion of flying along the world; that was by means of navigation; there, they said, a man did not tremble, and was not soiled or delayed by the mud, and he could fly from one end of the world to the other, finding everywhere something new, unseen and unheard of; and they lead me to the boundary of the land, where we could see nothing before us but sky and water.

(*Description of a Ship.*)

12. Then they bade me enter a little hut constructed out of planks; and this did not stand on the earth, neither had it a foundation, nor was it strengthened by any ceiling, beams, columns, or props; but it stood on the water and rocked to and fro, so that one had even to enter it with prudence. But as others went there I also went, not to appear timid, for they said that this was our carriage. But while I thought that we should proceed, or rather, as they

said, immediately fly on, we remained where we were on the second, the third, the tenth day. " What, then, is this ? " quoth I. " Did you then not tell me that we should fly directly from one end of the earth to the other ? and now we cannot by any means leave this spot." They then said we should wait till the relays came, and that they had relays which required neither shelter nor stable, nor forage, nor spurs, nor whip; they had only to put them to, and to drive on; I should but wait and I would see. Meanwhile, they show me cords, ropes, traces, scales, gambrels, shafts, axle-trees, waggon-beams, poles and various levers; and all these articles were fashioned in a manner different from that of the waggoners' carts. It was a cart that lay backwards, and had at its back shafts (consisting of two very long pine-trees), which projected high up into the air; from the top ropes descended to the sail-yards with various lattice-work and ladders. The axle-tree of the cart was at the back, and a man who sat there alone boasted that he could guide this huge mass in whatever direction he wished.

(Description of Navigation.)

13. Meanwhile the wind arose. Our crew started up; they begin to run to and fro, to jump, to scream, to shout; one seized this thing, another that; some climbed rapidly up and down the ropes, let down poles, expanded what seemed to be rush mats,[1] and

---

[1] I.e., sails; comp. More's " Utopia ": " The sayles were made of great rushes or of wickers."

other such things. Then, "What is this?" I said. They answered that they were putting to; and lo! I see that these rush mats swell out to the size of barns (they said these were our wings), and then everything above us begins to whizz, while under us the water is divided and splashes; and before I could look, the coast, and the land, and everything vanishes from our sight. "Whither, then, have we gone?" I said. "What now will befall us?" They said that we were flying. "Well, then, in the name of God, let us fly," I said, and I marvel how rapidly we move on, not indeed without pleasure, but also not without fear; for when I went above to look around me, giddiness overcame me; when I crawled below, the terror of the waves that rushed violently against the planks of the ship encircled me. And then I thought in my mind whether it was not grave foolhardiness to entrust a man's life to such furious elements as water and wind, and thus purposely to encounter death, from which we are separated by the breadth of two fingers; for no thicker is the plank which is between us and the terrible abyss. But having resolved not to allow my fear to be known, I was silent.

(*Disgust at Sea.*)

14. Then what seemed a crude form of stench begins to stun me, and penetrating my brain and all intestines, it prostrates me. Then I (as well as the others who were not used to these ways) roll about, scream, know no counsel; everything flows

from me and pours out of me, so that it appeared
to me, not otherwise, as if we were being dissolved
in the waters like snails in the sun.   Then I begin
to accuse myself and my guides, not believing it
possible that I should remain living; but from
them, instead of pity, I obtained but mockery.
No doubt they knew from experience (what I
knew not) that this trouble would not endure
more than a few days; and thus it was, and
my strength gradually returned, and I understood
that the furious sea had only welcomed me thus.

(*Calm on the Sea.*)

15. But what of this ?   Worse things than these
soon befell us. The wind left us, our wings became
flabby ; we stopped, unable to go anywhere.   I
again begin to knit my brow, wondering what
would happen. "We have been driven into these
deserts of the sea.   Oh, shall we ever leave them
again ?   Oh, shall we ever again see the lands of
the living ?   Oh, my mother, dear earth ! oh, dear
earth, my mother, where art thou ?   God, the
Creator, gave the water to the fishes, but thee to
us.   Alas ! the fishes prudently remain in their
dwelling-place, but we senselessly forsake ours.
If Heaven cometh not to our help, we must certainly perish in this doleful abyss."   Over these
distressful thoughts my soul did not cease to
grieve, till the sailors suddenly began to scream.
Running out, I exclaimed: "What is this ? "
They answered that the wind was rising; and I

look and see nothing. Yet they spread out the
sails; and the wind comes, seizes us, and carries
us along. This gave great pleasure to all, but the
pleasure soon became bitter.

(*Storm at Sea.*)

16. The wind meanwhile had increased so
rapidly that not only we, but also the waves
beneath us, were tossed about, so that terror
entered our hearts. The sea rolled round us in
every direction with such gigantic waves that our
course was up high hills and down deep valleys, now
upward, then downward. Sometimes we were shot
upwards to such heights that it seemed as if we
were to reach the moon; then again we descended
as into an abyss. Now it appeared as if a wave,
coming either straight or sideways towards us,
would surprise us, and immediately drown us; but
it merely lifted us on high, only that this our
barque was thrown about here and there, and
tossed on from one wave to another; sometimes
it declined to this side, sometimes to that; sometimes with its prow it went perpendicularly
upward, sometimes downward. Therefore, not
only was the water spirted skyward on us and
above us, but we could neither stand nor lie; we
were tossed from side to side, and found ourselves
sometimes on our feet, sometimes on our head.
This caused giddiness and the subversion of everything within us.[1] And as this continued both by

[1] *I.e.*, sea-sickness.

day and by night, everyone can conceive what
anguish and fear we felt. Then I said to myself: "Surely these seafaring men must be more
pious than all other men in the world, they who
never for an hour are sure of their lives?" But
looking at them, I observed that they were all,
without exception, eating gluttonously as in a
tavern—drinking, playing, laughing, talking in
an obscene manner; in fact, committing every
sort of evil deed and licentiousness. Grieving at
this, I begin to admonish them, and to beg them
to remember where we were, and ceasing such
things, to call unto God. But what avails it? Some
laughed; others scoffed at me; others struck
out at me; others wanted to throw me over-
board. My guide Falsehood told me to be silent,
and to remember that I was in a strange house,
where it is best to be deaf and blind. "Oh, it
is impossible," quoth I, "that this matter should
end well when they have such customs!" Then
they again laughed. Seeing such mischievousness, I
was obliged to be silent, for I feared to receive a
whipping from them.

(*The Ship is submerged.*)

17. At this moment the storm became stronger,
and a terrible gale burst on us. Then, indeed, the
sea, with its waves, begins to rise heavenward; then
the waves pass us on from one to another as if we
were balls; then the depths open up, and sometimes threaten to devour us, sometimes again toss

us downward; then the wind, encircling us, drives
us hither and thither, so that everything crashed as
if the ship was going to be shattered into a hundred
thousand pieces. Then I became as one dead, and
saw nothing before me but destruction. But the
sailors, who could no longer resist the violence of
the storm, and feared to be driven on to rocks
or shallows, pulled down the wings, and by means
of thick ropes threw out large iron hooks, hoping
thus to remain on the same spot till the storm
should have ceased. But in vain! Some of the
men who climbed along the ropes were shaken off
them by the wind as if they had been caterpillars,
and thrown into the sea; also through the force of
the waves the anchors were broken off and sank
into the depths. And then at last our ship, and we
with it, began to drift about helplessly like a chip
of wood in a stream. Then only did those iron,
wilful giants lose heart; they became pale,
trembled, knew not what to do; then only remembered God, exhorted us to pray, and they
also wrung their hands. Then our ship begins to
sink down to the bottom of the sea, to strike
against rocks concealed under the water, and thus
to sink and break up; then through fissures water
flows towards us; and though all, young and old,
were ordered to pour out the water with all their
might, this availed them not; it pressed powerfully
against us, and drew us to it. Then there were
tears, screams, moaning without measure. No one
saw anything before him but a cruel death. But
as life is sweet, everyone seized what he could—

tables, planks, poles, hoping that they could save themselves from drowning and swim forth to some spot.

And when at last the ship broke up and everything was submerged, then I also, seizing what I could, arrived at some coast, with a few others. The terrible abyss had devoured all the others. When I had somewhat recovered from my fear and horror, I begin to rebuke my guides that they had led me here. They said that this would not harm me ; now that we had escaped, I should be of a cheerful mind. A cheerful mind, indeed! To the day of my death I shall not allow myself to be led into anything of this sort.

18. Then looking round, I see that those who had been saved with me again ran to the shore and entered a ship. " Go, then, to encounter all misfortunes, ye foolhardy men," I said. " I cannot even look at this." My interpreter said: " Not everyone is so effeminate. Possessions and merchandise, my good fellow, are a fine thing. To obtain these, a man must ever risk his life." Then I said : "Am I, then, a beast, that I should risk my life merely for the sake of my body, and for the purpose of collecting things for it? Verily, indeed, even the beasts do not this, and man, possessing within him a superior thing, namely, the soul, should seek rather its advantage and pleasure."

H

CHAPTER X

THE PILGRIM BEHOLDS THE FATE OF THE MEN OF
LEARNING, AT FIRST GENERALLY

AND my guide said unto me, "I already now
understand thy mind, and which way it tendeth.
Go, then, among the learned men—go among the
learned. Their life hath a charm for thee; it is
easier, quieter, and more useful to thy mind."
"Yes, that is true," said the interpreter; "for what
could be more delightful than that a man should,
abandoning and no longer heeding the struggles of
this material life, employ himself in studying these
manifold beautiful things? Verily, it is this that
makes mortal men like unto the immortal God, and
almost equal to Him; thus do they become almost
omniscient, exploring everything that is in heaven, or
earth, or the depths, or was or will be. And thus do
they know everything, although not everyone, it is
true, receives these gifts in equal perfection." "Lead
me then there," I said. "Why dost thou tarry?"

(A Rigid Examination at first.)

2. And we arrived at a gate which they named
"Disciplina," and this was long, narrow, and dark.

It was full of armed guards, to whom everyone who entered the street of the learned men had to render account; also had he to ask of them a safe conduct. And I saw what crowds of people, mostly young ones, came up, and immediately underwent divers severe examinations. Each one was first examined as to what pouch, what posteriors, what head, what brain (of this they judged by the secretions from the nostrils[1]) and what skin he had. If, then, the head was of steel, the brain in it of quicksilver, the posteriors leaden, the skin iron, and the pouch golden, then these men were praised, and incontinently gladly conducted farther. But if one did not possess these five things, they either ordered him to retire or, though foreboding evil, they admitted him at random. And wondering at this, I said: "Why, then, do they lay such stress on these five metals that they search for them so industriously?" "They have great value indeed," quoth the interpreter. "If one has not a head of steel it will burst; if he has not within it a brain of liquid quicksilver, he will not obtain in it a looking-glass;[2] if he has not a skin of tin he will not be able to endure the toil of education; if he has not leaden posteriors he will not be able to endure the sedentary life of the student, and will indeed lose everything; and without a golden pouch whence could a man obtain leisure, whence masters living and dead? Or dost thou think those things can be

[1] According to the ideas of Komensky's time, these were believed to be secretions of the brain.

Komensky thus allegorically describes the imagination.

procured without cost?" And I understood the drift of his words, namely, that for the state of the learned, health, talent, consistency, patience, and gold are necessary. Then I said: "Truly can it be spoken, 'Non cuivis con tingit adire Corinthum'" (Not all wood becomes strong).[1]

(The Entrance to Study is difficult and painful. Memoria Artificialis.)

3. And we pass on through the gate, and I see that each one of these guards sets tasks to one or more of these men, and directed them. Now he whispers something into their ears, wipes their eyes, cleanses their noses and nostrils, pulls out and clips their tongues, folds together and then disjoins their hands and fingers; and I know not what else he did not. Some also endeavoured to pierce into their heads and to pour something into them. Then my interpreter, seeing me afraid, said: "Wonder not; learned men must have their hands, tongues, eyes, ears, brain, and internal and external senses different from the foolish herd of men; therefore must they here be transformed, and without trouble and offence this cannot be." Then I gaze, and behold how dearly these wretched ones had to pay for their transformation. I speak not of their pouches, but of their skins, which had to suffer; for fists, canes, sticks, birch rods struck them on their cheeks, heads, backs, and posteriors till blood streamed forth, and they were almost

[1] Literally musculous.

entirely covered with stripes, scars, spots, and weals. Some, seeing this, turned backward before entrusting themselves to these guards; and, indeed, as soon as they had looked through the gate, others wishing to escape from such educators also fled. A smaller number only remained, until they were allowed to return into the open air; and feeling a desire for this instruction, I also remained, though not without difficulty and bitterness.

(A Device is given to each Learned Man.)

4. When we pass through the gate, I see that to each one of those whose wit had been somewhat sharpened they gave a badge, by which it could be known that he was one of those who were learned. This was an inkstand at the girdle, a pen in the ear, and in the hand an empty book for the purpose of seeking knowledge. And I also received these things. Then Searchall said to me : " Now, here have we fourfold crossways leading to philosophy, medicine, jurisprudence, and theology ; where shall we go first ? " " As you judge," quoth I. Then he again said: " Let us first go into the market-place, where all assemble ; there canst thou behold them all together ; then will we proceed through the various lecture-rooms."

(Among the Learned also there are Deficiencies.)

5. And my guide leads me into the market-place ; and behold, there were clouds of students, masters,

doctors, priests, youths, and grey-headed men. Some of these stood together conversing and disputing ; others betook themselves to corners, so as to be out of the view of the rest. Some (as I well saw, but I dared not speak to them of this) had eyes, but had no tongue ; others had a tongue, but had no eyes : others had only ears, but neither eyes nor tongue ; and so forth. Thus did I understand that here also defects remained. But as I now see that all these men enter into the place, and then again leave it, as bees swarm into and out of a bee-hive, I insist that we also should go there.

(*Description of a Library.*)

6. Thus we enter ; and behold, there was a hall so large that I could not perceive its ending, and on all sides it was so full of many shelves, compartments, and gallipots that a man could not have conveyed them on a hundred thousand carts ; and each one had its own inscription and title. And I said : " What apothecary's shop have we then entered ? " " Into an apothecary's shop," said the interpreter, " where remedies against the ailments of the mind are kept; and this, by its proper name, is called a library. See what endless storehouses of wisdom are here." Then looking, I see long rows of learned men, who arrived from all directions and turned round these things. Some chose out the finest and most subtle among them, extracted morsels from them, and received them into their bodies, gently chewing and digesting

them. Approaching one of these men, I ask him,
"What is done here?" He answered me: "I
improve."[1]   "And what taste is there in this?"
quoth I.   And he again: "As long as a man
chews it in the mouth, he feels bitterness and
sourness, but afterwards it changes into sweetness."
"And wherefore is this?" I said. He answered:
"It is easier for me to carry this within me; also
am I thus surer. Dost thou then not see the use?"
I looked at him with more care, and I see that he
is stout and fat and of comely colour. His eyes
glittered like candles; his speech was careful, and
everything about him was lively. Then my
interpreter says: "Let us see these others also."

(*Disorder in the Studies.*)

And I gaze, and lo! some here bore themselves
most greedily, cramming down constantly everything that came into their hands. Then looking
at them more carefully, I see that their colour, their
body, and their fat had by no means increased, and
that their bellies only were swollen and puffed out.
I see also that what they crammed down again
crept out of them undigested either above or below.
Giddiness also befell some of these men, or they
maddened; others became pale, pined away and
died. Seeing this, others pointed at them and told
each other how dangerous it was to deal with books
(for this was the name they gave to these gallipots);
some fled, others exhorted each other to handle

[1] *I.e.*, my mind.

them carefully. These, therefore, did not absorb everything; rather did they burden themselves in front and behind with bags and pouches into which they crammed these gallipots (on most of them they saw written—"Vocabulary, Dictionary, Lexicon Promptuarium, Floriligium, Loci Communes Postillæ, Concordancy Herbal," and so forth, according to what each one judged appropriate); these they carried with them, and when they had to speak or write something they took them from their pouches, and put them in their mouth or pen. Noting this, I said: "These, then, carry their learning in their pockets?" The interpreter answered: "These are Memoriæ Subsidia; hast thou not heard of them?" I had, indeed, heard this custom praised by some; they said that those only who used them brought forth learned things. And it may be thus, but I noted other incommodities also. It befell in my presence that some scattered and lost their gallipots, while those of others caught fire while they had put them aside. Oh, how they then ran to and fro, wrung their hands, lamented, and cried for help! Now no one for a while wished to dispute, write, or preach any longer; they walked along drooping their heads, and bending downward and blushed, and endeavoured wherever they could to obtain another little box, either by means of entreaties or of money. Those, however, who had a store within them feared not such accidents so much.

(Students who study not.)

8. Meanwhile, I see others, again, who did not put these gallipots into their pouches, but carried them into a little chamber ; entering behind them, I see that they fit out beautiful cases for them, paint them in various colours, sometimes even border them with silver and gold, place them in shelves, and then drawing them out again, look at them ; then they fold and again unfold them, and walking to and fro, they show one another how beautiful these things are ; all this superficially. Some also at times looked at the titles, so that they might be able to name them. " Why, then," quoth I, " do these men trifle in this childish fashion ? " The interpreter answered : " Dear comrade, it is a fine thing to have a fine library." " Even if you use it not ? " said I. He answered : " Those also who love their libraries are counted among the learned." I thought within myself : " Just as those who own a large number of hammers and tongs, but know not how to use them, are counted among the blacksmiths." But I dared not to say this, fearing that they should give me foul word.

(Disorder in the Writing of Books.)

9. Then when we had again entered the hall, I see that in every direction the number of these gallipots increased, and I watched to see whence they brought them ; and I see that they were

brought from behind a screen. Going also behind it, I see many turners, who—one more diligently and neatly than the other—fashion these gallipots out of wood, bone, stone, and other materials ; then they fill them with salve or theriac, and deliver them up for general use. And the interpreter said to me : " These are the men worthy of praise and all honour, who serve their race in the most useful fashion, who regret no labour, no endeavours, which tend to increase wisdom and learning, and who share their glorious gifts with others. And the wish befell me to examine out of what stuff and in what manner these things (which the interpreter called gifts and wisdom) were made and fashioned. And I see one or two who collected fragrant roots and plants, cut them up, shook, cooked, and distilled them, preparing delightful theriacs, electuaries, syrups and other medicines, which are useful to the life of man. On the other hand, I saw some who only picked out things from the gallipots of others and transferred them into their own ; and of these there were hundreds. And I said : " These merely pour out water." The interpreter answered : " Thus also is learning increased ; for cannot one and the same thing be done now in this, now in that fashion ? Something can always be added to the first elements, and they can be thus improved." " And spoilt also," I said with anger, seeing plainly that deceit was being practised here. Some also, seizing the gallipots of others, filled up their own, and diluted the contents as much as they could, even by pouring in slops ;

another again condensed the mixture by adding every sort of hodge-podge, even dust and sweepings, so that it appeared to be freshly made up. Then they erected inscriptions that were even more pompous than those of the others, and like other quacks, each one impudently praised his own wares. Then I both wondered and angered that (as I said before) hardly ever did anyone examine the internal substance; rather did they take everything, or at least without choice ; and if some did indeed choose, they only contemplated the outward appearance and the inscription.[1] And then I understood why so few attained the inward freshness of the mind ; for the more of these medicines each man devoured, the more he vomited, turned pale, faded and decayed. And I saw also that a large number of these delightful medicaments were not even used by men, but became the portion of moths, worms, spiders, and flies, and were lost in the midst of dust and mould in dark presses and remote corners.

Fearing this fate, some, as soon as they had prepared their theriac (some, indeed, before they had begun to prepare it), ran to their neighbours asking them for prefaces, verses, anagrams; they instantly searched for patrons, who should lend their names and purses to the new preparations; they instantly wrote the title and inscription in the most ornate fashion ; they instantly embellished the divers figures and engravings with curling flowers; also they themselves carried them among the people,

[1] This, of course, refers to the binding and lettering of books.

and, so to speak, thrust them even on those who were reluctant to receive them. But I saw that this also availed not, for everywhere the market was overstocked. And I pitied some who, although they could have enjoyed simple quiet, yet gave themselves to this quackery without any necessity or use, and, indeed, at the risk of their good name, and to the harm of their neighbours. But when I gave news of this I earned but hatred, as if I had injured the common welfare. I am silent as to how some prepared these their electuaries out of materials that were plainly poisonous, so that as many poisons as medicaments were sold; and unwillingly did I bear such a misdeed, but there was no one who could have set matters right.

(*Discord and Strife.*)

10. Then we again enter the market-place of the learned, and behold, there were quarrels, strife, scuffles, tumult among them. Rarely was there one who had not a squabble with another; for not only the young ones (with whom it could be imputed to the insolence of undeveloped youth), but even the old men plundered one another. For the wiser one considered himself, or was by others held to be, the more he began to quarrel with those around him, fought and hacked, threw and shot at them, till it was fearful to behold; and he founded his honour and glory on this. And I said: " But in the name of dear God, what is this? I had thought, and this was it promised me by you, that

this was the most peaceful career." The interpreter answered : " My son, thou dost not understand this ; these men only sharpen their wits."
" What! thou sayest they sharpen their wits!
But I see wounds, and blood, and wrath, and
murderous hate of the one against the other. Not
even among the class of traders have I witnessed
anything similar." "No doubt," he said, " for the
arts of such men are but handicrafts, and are
slavish, while those of the others are free. Therefore what is not allowed and would not be permitted to them, the others have full liberty to do."
" But how this can be called order," I said, " I know
not." It is true that apparently their arms
seemed by no means terrible. For the spears,
swords, and daggers with which they hacked and
stabbed one another were of leather, and they held
them not in the hand but in the mouth. Their
artillery consisted of reeds and quills, which they
loaded with powder that had been dissolved in
water, and they then threw paper bullets at each
other. Nothing of this, say I, viewed superficially,
appeared terrible ; but when I saw that if a man
was even slightly struck he was convulsed,
screamed, reeled, fled, it was easy for me to understand that this was not jesting, but veritable
warfare. Sometimes many pressed one hardly, till
everywhere around the noise of swords danged in
the ears, and paper bullets fell on him like hail.
Sometimes a man, fighting bravely, defended himself and dispersed the aggressors ; another, again,
overcome by his wounds, fell to the ground. And

I beheld here cruelty unusual elsewhere, for they spared neither the wounded nor the dead ; indeed, they hacked and struck all the more unmercifully at him who could no longer defend himself, mostly endeavouring to show their valour in this fashion. Some, indeed, dealt with each other in a more moderate manner ; but these, also, were not free from disputes and misunderstandings. For no sooner had one given out an opinion than another straightly contradicted it ; they disputed even as to whether snow was white or black, fire hot or cold.

(*Great Confusion among them.*)

11. Meanwhile, some interfered in these disputes and began to counsel peace, and I joined these men. It was also said that all disputes would now be settled, and the question arose, Who was to undertake this ? The answer was that by permission of Queen Wisdom, the wisest of all classes were to be selected, and power given unto them— after hearing the adverse parties—to discriminate among the divers opinions with regard to all things, and to proclaim what opinion was the true one. And many crowded together who either were to be or wished to be judges ; of those, in particular, who had had dissensions because of the differences of their views, a large number assembled. Among these I saw Aristotle with Plato, Cicero with Sallustius, Scotus [1] with Aquinas, [2] Bartolus

---

[1] *I.e.*, John Duns Scot.
[2] *I.e.*, St. Thomas of Aquinas.

with Baldus, Erasmus with the men of the
Sorbonne, Ramus and Campanella with the peri-
patetics, Theophrastus with Galenus, Hus, Luther
and others with the Pope and the Jesuits,
Brentius [1] with Beza, Bodinus [2] with Wier, [3]
Sleidanus [4] with Surius, [5] Schmidlin [6] with the
Calvinists, Gomarus with Arminius, the Rosicrucians with philosophasters, [7] and countless
others. When the mediators ordered them to
bring forward their accusations and complaints in
writing, and compressed into as few words as
possible, they laid down such piles of books that
six thousand years would not have been sufficient
to examine them ; and they asked that this summary of their views should for the time be accepted, but that each one should have full liberty,
later, when the necessity showed itself, to more fully
explain and expound his views. And they began
to look at these books, and as soon as a man began
to look at one of them he became, as it were,

---

[1] John Brentius or Brenz, was one of the German
Church Reformers of the sixteenth century.

[2] John Bodinus, a French writer of the sixteenth century.

[3] Josef Wier, born 1515, was a celebrated physician and
writer, noted for his controversies with Bodin.

[4] John Sleidanus, whose real name was Philipson, was an
historian of the sixteenth century.

[5] Lawrence Surius, born at Lubeck in 1522, of Protestant
parents, became a Roman Catholic, and was the author of
theological works that were celebrated at the time
Komensky wrote.

[6] Jacob Schmidlin, born 1528 at Weiblingen, was a note-
worthy Protestant theologian.

[7] *I.e.*, false philosophers.

intoxicated, and attempted to defend it.[1]   Among the arbitrators and mediators also great dissension began, for one man maintained this opinion, another that one.   And having thus settled nothing, they dispersed, and the learned men again returned to their quarrels ; and this grieved me unto tears.

[1] *I.e.*, its contents.

CHAPTER XI

THE PILGRIM COMES AMONG THE PHILOSOPHERS PUBLICLY

THEN my interpreter said: "Now I will lead you among the philosophers, whose work it is to remedy the deficiencies of men, and to show wherein true wisdom consisteth." Then I said: "Here at least I shall, thank God, learn something certain." He said: "Assuredly, for these are men who know the truth of everything; without their knowledge neither does heaven do anything nor the abyss conceal anything; they nobly guide the lives of men to virtue; they enlighten communities and lands. They have God for a friend, and by means of their wisdom penetrate His mysteries." "Let us go," I said; "let us go among them as soon as possible." But when he led me there, and I saw a large number of old men and their wondrous follies, I was amazed. There I beheld Bion sitting down quietly; there Anacharsis walked to and fro, Thales flew, Hesiod ploughed, Plato hunted in the skies for ideas, Homer sang, Aristotle disputed, Pythagoras was silent, Epimenides slept, Archimedes moved the earth,[1] Solon wrote laws and Galen prescriptions, Euclid measured the hall, Kleobulus inquired into the future, Periander measured out their duties to men, Pittacus warred, Bias begged, Epictetus served, Seneca praised poverty while surrounded by tons of gold, Socrates informed everyone that he knew nothing; Xenophon, on the contrary, promised to teach everyone everything; Diogenes, peeping out of a tub, insulted all who passed by; Timon cursed all, Democritus laughed at all this; Heraclitus, on the other hand, cried; Zeno fasted, Epicure feasted; Anaxarchus said that all things were nothing in reality, but only appeared to exist. Of other little philosophers there were many, and each one endeavoured to prove something particular; and I did not remember everything, nor do I wish to be reminded of it all. Pondering over this, I said : "These, then, are the wise men, the lights of the world. Alas, alas! I had hoped for other things; here, as peasants in a tavern, each one screams, and each one differently.' The interpreter said to me : " Thou art a fool; thou dost not understand these mysteries." Then behold, some one stepped up to us, also in the garb of a philosopher (he was called Paul of Tarsus) and he said into mine ear: "If anyone thinks himself wise in this world, let him first be simple, so that he may become wise. Assuredly the wisdom of this world is folly before God. For it is written:

---

[1] An obvious allusion to Archimedes' well-known remark to Hiero, which in the Latin version runs thus : " Da mihi punctum et terram movebo."

'The Lord knoweth the thoughts of the wise that they are vain'" (1. Cor. chap. iii., verse 20). But as I saw from this speech that it agreed with what my eyes and ears saw and heard, I willingly acquiesced in this, and " Let us go elsewhere," I said. My interpreter then blamed my folly, for that, though able to learn something from these wise men, I yet fled them. None the less I silently went my way.

(The Pilgrim comes among the Grammarians.)

2. And we entered into a lecture-room which, behold, was full of men, young and old, who with pencils drew letters, lines and points; and if one wrote down a thing or pronounced it differently from another, they either derided one another or quarrelled. Then they placed words on the walls, and disputed about them as to which one should precede the other; and then they composed, disposed, and transplaced them in various fashions. And wondering at this, and seeing no meaning in it, I said: " These are childish things; let us go elsewhere."

(Among the Rhetoricians.)

3. We then came to another hall, where, behold, many stood holding brushes, and they discussed as to how words either written or spoken into the air could be coloured green, red, black, white, or whatever colour a man might wish. And I asked what

was the purpose of this. I was told in answer that it was done that the brains of the listeners might be coloured in this fashion or that. I again said: "Is it for portraying truth or lies that they use these colours?" The interpreter answers: "It is as it happens." "Then there is here as much falsehood and vanity as truth and profit," say I; and I go from there.

(*Among the Poets.*)

4. Then we arrive elsewhere, and behold, here was a troop of agile young men who were weighing syllables on balances, and measuring them by the span, rejoicing meanwhile, and skipping round them. And I marvelled what this was, and the interpreter said to me: "Of all the arts that spring from letters, none is more skilful or gayer than this." "And what, then, is it?" quoth I. He answered: "That which cannot be said in simple speech can be expressed in these their compositions." But seeing that those who were learning this art of composing words looked into certain books, I look also, and see names such as "De Culice," "De Passere," "De Lesbia," "De Priapo," "De Arte Armandi," "Metamorphoses," "Encomia," "Satyræ," and generally farces, poems, love passages, and amatory trifling of every sort. Then was I again disgusted with the whole matter; particularly when I saw that whoever flattered these measurers of syllables, him they endeavoured in every fashion to further. But if one was not agreeable to them,

at him they threw sneers from all directions, so
that they used their art only either to flatter or to
sting. Having now remarked what passionate folk
they were, I gladly turned away from them.

(*Among the Logicians.*)

5. Then proceeding onward, we enter another
building where they manufactured and sold spy-
glasses. I asked : "What is this ? " The answer
was that these were "Notiones secundæ," and that
he who had them perceived everything, not superficially only, but also to the innermost core; particularly one man could see into the brain of another
and sift his mind. And many came forward and
purchased these glasses, and masters taught them
how to fasten them on, and, if necessary, how to
turn them. The masters, then, who made them
were peculiar in this, that they had their workshops in remote corners. But they did not make
them uniform; one made small, another large ones,
one round, the other square ones, and each one
praised his own wares and enticed the buyers, and
they quarrelled implacably, and pelted one another.
Some purchased glasses from all the dealers and
placed them on their noses; others chose only one
and fixed it on. Then some said that they yet
could not see far; others said they could see, and
showed each other their innermost brain and
intellect. But I saw that of these not a few, when
they began to step forward, fell over stones and
blocks or into pits (of such things, as I have

already said, there were many). And I asked: "How, then, is it that though everything can be seen through these spectacles, they yet do not avoid such shocks ? " It was answered me that this was the fault, not of the spectacles, but of those who knew not how to use them. The masters then said it was not sufficient to have the spectacles of dialectics, but that the view must also be cleared by a clear eye-salve composed of physics and mathematics; therefore should these proceed to other lecture-rooms and strengthen their eyesight. And I to my guides: " Let us also go there." But I did not succeed in this before, induced by Searchall, I had procured and fastened on some of these spectacles. And it seemed to me that it was true that I saw somewhat more, and that some things could be viewed in divers fashions. But I continually insisted that we should proceed so that I might try the eye-salve of which they spoke.

(*Among the Natural Philosophers.*)

6. And we proceeded, and they led me to a square, in the middle of which I see a large wide-spreading tree on which grew sundry leaves and sundry fruits (all, as it were, in the shell); they told me that this was Nature. Round it there was a crowd of philosophers examining it, and expounding to one another how each of the branches, leaves, and fruits should be named. And I said : " I hear that these men learn how to name things, but that they comprehend Nature I do not as yet see." The

interpreter answered me : " Not everyone can be able to do that; but look at these." And I saw some who broke off branches, unrolled the leaves and fruit, and when they came to the nuts, gnawed at them till their teeth shook; but they said that they thus broke the shells, and, picking them up, boasted that they had obtained the kernel; and they showed it secretly to some, but only to few. But taking a careful view of them, I saw clearly that they had, indeed, broken and crushed the outward rind and bark, but that the hardest shell in which the kernel lay embedded was intact. Then seeing here also vain ostentation and idle striving (for some, indeed, stared till their eyes pained them, and gnawed till they broke their teeth), I proposed that we should go elsewhere.

(*Among the Metaphysicians—Unum verum bonum.—*
P. Ramus.)[1]

7. Then we enter another hall, and behold here, these philosophical gentlemen—having before them cows, donkeys, wolves, serpents, and various wild animals, birds and reptiles, as well as wood, stones, water, fire, clouds, stars and planets, and even angels—disputed as to how each creature could be deprived of that which distinguished it from the others, so that all should become similar; and they

[1] Ramus or La Ramée, the well-known French philosopher, born 1515, killed in Paris on St. Bartholomew's Day (1572). Komensky greatly valued his writings, as being opposed to the teaching of Aristotle.

took from them first the shape, then the material, at last all accessories, so that at last the mere ens remained. And then they disputed as to whether all things were one and the same, whether all things are verily that which they are; and they asked each other more questions such as these. Noticing this, some began to wonder, and to tell how high human wit had risen, so that it was able to surpass all creatures, and to divest all corporal things of their corporality. At last I also began to delight in these subtleties. But then, one rising up declared that such things were mere phantasies, and they should desist from them. And he drew some away with him; but others, again, arose and condemned him as a heretic, saying that he separated men from philosophy, which is the highest knowledge, and, as it were, the head " artium." And after listening sufficiently to these disputes, I went away from this spot.

(*Among the Arithmeticians.*)

8. And proceeding on our way, we come among some who dwelt in a hall full of ciphers, and shifted them carefully. Some took a few from the lot and placed them differently; others, again, collected these separate portions into one; others, again, divided them and spread them out, so that I wondered at this their work. Meanwhile, they said that in all philosophy there was no knowledge more certain than theirs. Here, they said, there could be no mistakes, no errors, no superfluity.

" What, then, is the purpose of this science ? " I
said. They, wondering at my stupidity, began one
after the other to tell me marvellous tales. One
said he could tell me how many geese were flying
in a flock without counting them ; another said
he could tell in how many hours a cistern, flowing
out through five pipes, would empty itself. A third
man said he could tell me how many " groschen "
I had in my pouch without looking at it, and so
forth. Then at last one appeared who undertook
to count the sands of the sea, and immediately
wrote a book about this (Archimedes). Another,
following his example (but endeavouring to show
more subtlety), busied himself with counting the
atoms of dust that fly in the sun (Euclid). And I
was amazed ; and they, trying to assist me in
understanding this, said these men had laws called
" regulæ trium, societatis, alligationis, falsi." These
things I but dimly understood. But when they
wanted to teach me the deepest of all, which was
called Algebra or Cossa,[1] I saw such a heap of
weird and crooked writings that giddiness nearly
overcame me, and shutting my eyes, I begged that
I might be led elsewhere.

(*Among the Geometricians.*)

9. And we come to another lecture-room, over
which was written, " Ουδεις αγεωμέτρητος εισίτω,"

[1] From the Italian word "cosa," which the Italian mathe-
maticians of the sixteenth century used to designate the
unknown quantity.

and stopping, I said: "Shall we be allowed to enter here, for they admit only geometricians?" "Go on, none the less," said Impudence, and we entered; and behold, there were many there who drew lines, hooks, crosses, circles, squares, and points, each one quietly and apart from the others. Then one walked up to another, and showed what he had drawn. One said that it should be different, and another that it was well done; and they disputed about this. But if one found some new line or hook, he exulted with joy, and calling the others together, showed it them. These then wondered, turned their fingers and heads round, and each returning to his own corner endeavoured to fashion something similar. One succeeded, but another did not, so that the whole hall, the floor, the walls, and the ceiling were full of lines, and they did not allow anyone to tread on them or to touch them.

(*Præcipua apud geometras controversia de quadrando circulo. John Scaliger[1]—John Clavius.[2]*)

10. Those who were the most learned among them assembled in the middle of the hall and strove at something with great labour; and then I saw that all the others waited with open mouths; and there was much talk as to this being more won-

[1] Besides his better-known philological work, John Justus Scaliger studied mathematics and algebra.

[2] Clavius—a Jesuit—was famous as a mathematician and astronomer. He was consulted by Pope Gregory XIII., when that pope established the calendar that bears his name.

drous than any subtlety in the whole world ; were
it but discovered, they said, nothing would any
longer be impossible. Now I, desirous to know
what this was, stepped up to them and saw that
they had between them a circle, and the question
was how a square could be fashioned out of it.
And when they had striven at this with inexpressible labour, they again stepped apart, advising
one another to meditate further on the matter.
Then, after a short while, one suddenly jumped up,
crying: " I have ; I have discovered the mystery ;
I have ! " And they all crowded round him, hasten-
ing to see and to wonder. And he carried a large
book in folio, which he showed them ; and there
were cries and exulting, such as is usual after a
victory. But another man soon stopped these
rejoicings. He cried out as largely as his voice did
permit, that they should not allow themselves to
be deceived, and that what was shown them was
not a square. He then placed a yet larger book
before them, turned all the supposed squares again
into circles, and mightily strove to prove that it
was impossible for any man to carry out what the
other man had attempted. Then all hung down
their heads, and returned to their lines and to their
books.

(Among the Land Surveyors.)

11. We then come to another hall, where they
sold fingers, spans, yards, fathoms, scales, measures,
levers, cranes, vices, and other such instruments ;

and the place was full of those who measured and weighed. Others, again, measured the hall itself; and almost everyone measured it differently. Then they quarrelled and measured afresh. Some measured a shadow, as to its length, width, and breadth; others also weighed it in a balance. They said generally that there was nothing in this world nor out of it which they were unable to measure rightly. But having watched this their craft for some time, I observed that there was more boasting than use. Therefore, shaking my head, I proceeded elsewhere.

(*Among the Musicians.*)

12. And we come to another chamber which, as I perceive, was full of music and song, and strumming, and the sound of divers instruments; and there were some who stood around, who looked from above, from below, and inclined their ears, wishing to discover what the sound was, where it was, whence and whereto it came, why it was sometimes in tune and sometimes not. Some said that they already knew this, and they rejoiced, saying that it was something divine, and a mystery greater than all mysteries; therefore they drew these things asunder, placed them together, and then transposed them with great pleasure and rejoicing. But in this but one of a thousand was successful; the others merely looked on. Then if one attempted to employ his hands also at such endeavours, then all creaked and scraped; and

this befell me also. Then when I saw that some
who appeared to be men of value held all this to
be but toying and waste of time, I went elsewhere.

(*Among the Astronomers.*)

13. Then Impudence led me up some steps to
what appeared a gallery. There I saw a crowd of
men who were making ladders, and setting them
up unto the sky; they then crawled up and
caught at the stars, and spread over them strings,
levels, rulers, weights and compasses ; and they
measured their courses. Then some, sitting down,
wrote rules concerning such matters as to where,
and when, and how stars must meet or diverge.
And I wondered at the boldness of these people
who dared thus to raise themselves, and to give
orders to the stars ; then, finding taste in this
noble science, I also began strenuously to catch
at the stars. But when I had but slightly busied
myself with such endeavours, I clearly saw that
the stars by no means danced in accordance with
the fiddles[1] of these men. They indeed remarked
this themselves, and named the " anomalitatem
cœli " as the cause of the evil. They endeavoured
to place the stars in order ; now this way, now
that. They even changed their places, tossing
some downward toward the earth, while they
raised others upward. Generally, they thus and
by other means imagined " Hypotheses," but
nothing verily seemed to avail.

[1] A proverbial expression in Bohemia.

(Among the Astrologers.)

14. Then some no longer climbed thus upward; rather did they, gazing from below, study what the constellations were. They then arranged triangles, quadrangles, hexagons, conjunctions, oppositions, and other aspects;[1] by means of these they predicted, either publicly to the world or privately to certain persons, fortune or misfortune; wrote prognostics, and distributed them among the people. Hence sometimes fear and terror arose among the people, sometimes gaiety; for some heeded them not, threw the prognostics into a corner, mocked the astrologers, saying that even without prognostics one could eat enough, drink enough, sleep enough. But it did not seem to me fitting to heed so one-sided a judgment, if but the art itself was a true one. But the more I watched them, the less certainty did I perceive. If one prediction came true, five again proved false. Understanding now that, even without stars, guessing is easy, and that guessing rightly obtains praise, and that guessing wrongly is excused, I considered it vain to be delayed by such matters.

(Among the Historians.)

15. And we enter yet another square, where, behold, I see something new. For there stood

---

[1] Terms of mediæval astrology. The relative positions of the planets, the sun, and the moon in the zodiac were called aspects, and it was believed that the fates of men could be ascertained through them.

here some who had certain curved, bent trumpets; one end of these they pressed over their
eyes, while they placed the other across their
shoulders on to their backs. When I asked what
this was, the interpreter said that these things
were eye-glasses, with which one could see behind
one's back. "For," quoth he, "one who wishes to
be a man must see not only that which is before
his feet, but he must heed also that which is passed
and is behind his back, so that he may from the
past learn the present and the future." And I,
thinking that this was a new thing (for assuredly
I knew not before of such crooked eye-glasses),
begged one of the men to lend me his instrument for a short time that I might gaze through
it; and some gave them to me, and oh, monstrous
thing! through each one the view was different.
Through one something appeared distant, through
another the same thing appeared close; through
one it appeared in this, through another in that,
colour; again, through a third this thing appeared
not at all. Thus did I ascertain that there was
nothing here that I could rely on; nor was it
certain that anything was really as it appeared,
and not coloured before the eyes according to the
fashion in which the eye-glasses were fitted on.
But I saw that each one of these men trusted his
own instrument thoroughly; thence arose much
dispute on many matters, and this pleased me
not.

(Among the Moralists and Politicians.)

16. When they now begin to lead me elsewhere,
I ask: " Will there not soon be an end of all these
learned men; for already I feel weary and anxious
from moving about among them." " The best
yet remaineth," said Impudence. And we enter
a certain hall that was full of pictures; those
on one side were pretty and very delightful, but
those on the other side of the hall were ugly and
misshapen. Philosophers walked round the pictures, not only looking at them, but also, by means
of colours, adding to the beauty of some and to the
ugliness of others. And I asked, " What is this? "
The interpreter answered: " Dost thou then not
see the inscriptions on their foreheads? " And leading me nearer he showed me inscriptions, such as
Fortitudo, Temperantia, Justitia, Concordia, Regnum, and so forth; and on the other side, Superbia,
Gula, Libido, Discordia, Tyrannis, and so forth.
The philosophers then begged and beseeched all
who came near them to love the pretty pictures and
to hate the ugly ones; and they praised the ones as
much as they could, while they abused and blamed
the others as much as they could. This pleased
me well, and I said: " Now do I here, at least, find
some who have wrought something that is worthy
of the race of men." But meanwhile, I perceive
that these dear admonishers took no greater interest
in the beautiful pictures than in the others, and,
indeed, feared them less than they did the beautiful

ones ; some, indeed, approached the ugly ones with great pleasure, and others beholding this, also turned towards them, and began to trifle and make merry with these monsters. And I said, with wrath: " Here, then, I see that folk (as Æsop's wolf said) say one thing and do another ; what their mouth praises, from that their mind flies ; and that which their tongue abhors, to that their heart inclines." " I presume, then, that thou seekest angels among men," said the interpreter chidingly. " Will anything, then, anywhere please thee ? Everywhere thou findest but wrong." Then I was silent and hung down my head, particularly as I saw that all the others also, who perceived that I watched them, gazed at me with disfavour. And leaving them there, I went outside.

CHAPTER XII

THE PILGRIM STUDIES ALCHEMY

AND Impudence said: "Now at least come here; I will lead thee there where can be found the summit of human wit, and such delightful labours that he who once applies himself to it cannot abandon it as long as he lives, because of the noble pleasure that it gives to the mind." And I begged him not to tarry, but to directly show this to me. And then he led me into what appeared to be a cellar; and behold, there were there several rows of hearths, small ovens, kettles, and divers glass-work, so that everything glittered; men hurried about carrying brushwood and spreading it out; then they blew on it, lighted it, and then again extinguished it, pouring out some substance and mixing it in various fashions. And I asked: "Who are these men, and what are they doing?" Impudence answered: "They are the most subtle philosophers, who accomplish that which the heavenly sun, with its heat, cannot in many years effect in the bowels of the earth; that is, to raise divers metals to their highest degree—to wit, to gold." "But wherefore is this?" I said; "for surely more iron and other metal is used than gold?"

" What a dolt thou art ! " he said ; " for gold is the most precious metal; he who has it fears not poverty.

(Lapis Philosophicus.)

2. " Besides this, the substance which changes metals into gold has other wondrous powers; that one also that it preserves bodily health in its wholeness up to death, and does not admit death (except after two or three hundred years). Indeed, he who would know how to use this substance could make himself immortal. For this lapis is nothing other than the seed of life, the essence and extract of the whole world, out of which animals, plants, metals, and the elements themselves take their being." And I was afeard, hearing such wondrous things, and "These, then, are immortal?" I said. "Not all succeed in finding this substance ; and those also who obtain it do not always know how to deal with it fitly." " I should endeavour," said I, " if I had this stone, to use it in such a fashion that death could not reach me ; and I should hope to have enough gold for myself and others. But whence, then, do they take this stone?" He answered : " It is prepared here." " In these small kettles ? " I said. " Yes."

(The Fortunes of Alchemists.)

3. Wishing such wishes, I thus pursue my way, looking at everything, at what was done and how,

and I see that all did not fare equally. One left his fire too cold, and the substance did not boil. Another kept it too hot, then his implements burst, and something evaporated. The man then said that the azoth [1] had escaped, and he burst into tears. Another, while pouring out the substance, spilt some of it, or mixed it wrongly, and damaged his eyes by the smoke, and was unable to observe the calcination and the clearing of the substance; or his eyes were so saturated with smoke that before he had sufficiently rubbed them the azoth had flown from him. Some also died from inhaling the smoke. And there were many of them who had not sufficient coals in their pouch; these had to run to others to borrow some; meanwhile the brew grew cold, and everything came to naught. And this accident was here very frequent, almost incessant. For though they admitted no one among them who had not a full pouch, yet each man's pouch dried up, as it were, so quickly that nothing remained in it, and he was obliged either to stop his work or to run elsewhere on borrowing intent.

4. And gazing at them, I said: "Of those who work here in vain I see many, but I see no one who obtains the stone. I see, indeed, that smelting gold and broiling the element of life, these men squander and dissolve both. But where are these with their masses of gold and their immortality?" He answered me thus: "This knowledge will not be revealed to thee, nor would I counsel these men to

[1] *I.e.*, nitrogen.

do so. So precious a thing must be preserved in secrecy. For if one of the great of the world should hear of such a man, he would wish to seize him and make him a prisoner for life. Therefore must these men be silent."

5. Meanwhile, I see that some of those who had been scorched were meeting together and listening to them. I hear that they were discussing the failure of their endeavours among themselves. One laid the blame on the philosophers, saying that they taught their art in too involved a fashion; another complained of the frailty of the glass implements; a third pointed to the untimely and unfavourable aspect[1] of the planets; a fourth was angry because of the earthly and dim ingredients in Mercury;[2] a fifth complained of the insufficient expenditure. On the whole, they had so many excuses that they knew not how to defend their art. I saw this. And then, as one after the other went out, I also went thence.

[1] See note, p. 137.
[2] *I.e.*, quicksilver.

CHAPTER XIII

THE PILGRIM BEHOLDS THE ROSICRUCIANS

(*Fama fraternitatis Anno* 1612, *Latine ac Germanice edita.*)

AND then immediately I hear in the market-place the sound of a trumpet, and looking back, I see one who was riding a horse and calling the philosophers together. And when these crowded round him in herds, he began to speak to them in fine language of the insufficiency of all free arts and of all philosophy; and he told them that some famous men had, impelled by God, already examined these insufficiencies, had remedied them, and had raised the wisdom of man to that degree which it had in Paradise before the fall of man. To make gold, he said, was one of the smallest of their hundred feats, for all Nature was bared and revealed to them; they were able to give to, or take from, each creature whatever shape they chose, according to their pleasure; he further said that they knew the languages of all nations, as well as everything that happened on the whole sphere of the earth, even in the new world, and that they were able to discourse with one another even at a distance of a

thousand miles. He said they had the stone,[1] and
could by means of it entirely heal all illnesses
and confer long life. For Hugo Alverda,[2] their
præpositus, was already 562 years old, and his
colleagues were not much younger. And though
they had hidden themselves for so many hundred
years, only working—seven of them—at the
amendment of philosophy, yet would they now no
longer hide themselves, as they had already brought
everything to perfection ; and besides this, because
they knew that a reformation would shortly befall
the whole world ; therefore openly showing themselves, they were ready to share their precious
secrets with everyone whom they should consider
worthy. If, then, one applied to them in whatever
language, and be it that he was of whatever nation,
each one would obtain everything, and none would
be left without a kind answer. But if one was
unworthy, and merely from avarice or frowardness
wished to secure these gifts, then he should obtain
nothing.

(*Varia de Fama Judicia.*)

2. Having said this, the messenger vanished. I
then, looking at these learned men, see that almost
all of them were frightened by this news. Meanwhile, they begin slowly to put their heads together
and to pass judgment, some in a whisper, some

---

[1] *I.e.*, Lapis philosophicus—the philosopher's stone.
[2] Hugo Alverda was—according to Komensky—the founder
of the Rosicrucians.

loudly, on this event. And walking, now here, now there, among them, I listen. And behold, some rejoiced exceedingly, not knowing for joy where to go to. They pitied their ancestors, because, during their lifetime, nothing such had happened. They congratulated themselves because perfect philosophy had been fully given unto them. Thus could they, without error, know everything; without want, have sufficient of everything; live for several hundred years without sickness and grey hair, if they only wished it. And they ever repeated: " Happy, verily happy, is our age." Hearing such speech I also began to rejoice, and to feel hopes that, please God, I also should receive somewhat of that for which they were longing. But I saw others who were absorbed in deep thought, and were in doubt as to what to think this. Were it but true what they had heard announced, they would have been glad; but these matters seemed to them obscure, and surpassing the mind of man. Others openly opposed these things, saying that they were fraud and deceit. If these reformers of philosophy had existed for hundreds of years, why, then, had they not appeared before ? If they were certain of what they affirmed, why, then, did they not appear boldly in the light, but express their opinions in the dark, and in corners, as if they were whizzing bats. Philosophy, they said, is already well established, and requires no reform. If you allow this philosophy to be torn from your hands, you will have none whatever. Others also reviled and cursed the reformers and declared them to be divinators, sorcerers, and incarnate devils.

(*Fraternitatem Ambientes.*)

3. Generally there was a noise everywhere in the market-place, and almost everyone burnt with the desire of obtaining these goods. Therefore not a few wrote petitions (some secretly, some openly), and they sent them, rejoicing at the thought that they also would be received into the association.[1] But I saw that to each one his petition, after all parts of it had been briefly scanned, was returned without an answer; and their joyful hope was changed to grief, for the unbelievers laughed at them. Some wrote again, a second, a third time, and oftener; and each man, through the aid of the muses,[2] begged, and even implored, that his mind might not be deprived of that learning which was worthy of being desired. Some, unable to bear the delay, ran from one region of the earth to another, lamenting their misfortune that they could not find these happy men. This one attributed to his own unworthiness; another to the ill-will of these men, and then one man despaired, while another, looking round and seeking new roads to find these men, was again disappointed, till I myself was grieved, seeing no end to this.

[1] *I.e.*, of the Rosicrucians.
[2] *I.e.*, through eloquence, poetry, and the liberal arts.

(Contumatio Famæ Rosæorum.)

4. Meanwhile, behold the blowing of trumpets again begins; then many, and I also, run in the direction from which the sound came, and I beheld one who was spreading out his wares and calling on the people to view and buy his wondrous secrets; they were, he said, taken from the treasury of the new philosophy, and would content all who were desirous of secret knowledge. And there was joy that the holy Rosicrucian brotherhood would clearly now share its treasures bounteously with them; many approached and bought. Now everything that was sold was wrapped up in boxes that were painted and had various pretty inscriptions, such as: Portæ Sapientiæ; Fortalitium Scientiæ; Gymnasium Universitatis; Bonum Macro-micro-cosmicon; Harmonia utriusque Cosmi; Christiano - Cabalisticum; Antrum Naturæ; Tertrinum Catholicum; Pyramis Triumphalis, and so forth.[1]

Now everyone who purchased was forbidden to open his box; for it was said that the force of this secret wisdom was such that it worked by penetrating through the cover; but if the box was opened it would evaporate and vanish. None the

---

[1] These words of uncouth Latinity form part of the vocabulary particular to the Rosicrucians, and Komensky has formed them partly on Paracelolus Venetus. Komensky was well acquainted with the tenets of the Rosicrucians, as Andreæ, whose pupil he was, and from whom—as noted elsewhere—part of the contents of the " Labyrinth " are derived, was one of the prominent Rosicrucians.

less, some of those who were more forward could not refrain from opening them, and finding them quite empty, showed this to the others; these then also opened theirs, but no one found anything. They then cried "Fraud! fraud!" and spoke furiously to him who sold the wares; but he calmed them, saying that these were the most secret of secret things, and that they were invisible to all but "filiis scientiæ" (that is, the sons of science); therefore if but one out of a thousand obtained anything, this was no fault of his.

(Eventus Famæ.)

5. And they mostly allowed themselves to be appeased by this. Meanwhile, the man took himself off, and the spectators, in very different humours, dispersed in divers directions; whether some of them ascertained something concerning these mysteries or not, I have hitherto been unable to learn. This only I know, that everything, as it were, became quiet. Those whom I had at first most seen running and rushing about, these I afterwards beheld sitting in corners with locked mouths, as it appeared; either they had been admitted to the mysteries (as some believed of them), and were obliged to carry out their oath of silence, or (as it seemed to me, looking without any spectacles), they were ashamed of their hopes and of their uselessly expended labour. Then all this dispersed and became quiet, as after a storm the clouds disperse without rain. And I said to my guide: "Is nothing, then, to come

of all this? Alas, my hopes! for I likewise, seeing
such expectations, rejoiced that I had found nurture
convenient to my mind." The interpreter answered:
" Who knows? Someone may yet succeed in this.
Perhaps these men know the hour when they
should reveal these things to someone." " Am I
then to wait for this?" I said. " I who, among so
many thousand who are more learned than I, know
not a single example of one who succeeded? I do
not wish to continue gaping here. Let us proceed
hence."

CHAPTER XIV

THE PILGRIM STUDIES MEDICINE

(*Anatomia.*)

THEN my guides, leading me between the physical and the chemical lecture-rooms, along some small streets, place me in another open space, where I beheld a fearful sight. They stretched a man out, and cutting off one of his limbs after the other, they examined all his intestines, and with great pleasure showed one another what they found discovered there. Quoth I : " What cruelty, then, is this, to deal with a man as if he were a beast ? " " It must be thus," said the interpreter. " This is their school."

(*Botanografia.*)

2. But these men had meanwhile abandoned this work, and they now ran in divers directions through gardens, meadows, fields, and hills ; whatever things they found growing there they plucked, and they carried together such heaps that many years would not have sufficed for merely sifting and examining them. And each one seized out of them what he thought good, or what came in his

way, and then ran back to the bodies which had
been cut up, and spread the herbs over the limbs,
measuring them together according to length, width,
breadth. One said that this fitted that, another
that it did not; then they wrangled about this
with much screaming—nay, even as to the very
names of these herbs there was much dispute.
Him who knew most names of herbs, and was
able to measure and weigh them, they crowned
with a garland of such herbs; and they ordered
that he should be called doctor of this science.

(*Praxis Medendi.*)

3. Then I perceive that they bring and carry to
these men many who, either inwardly or outwardly,
had wounds, and were purulent and rotten. Stepping towards them, they looked at their putrefied
limbs, smelt the stench that proceeded from them,
handled the filth that leaked out from above and
below till it was loathsome to behold. And this
they called examination. Then they immediately
cooked, stewed, roasted, broiled, cauterised, cooled,
burnt, hacked, sawed, pricked, sewed together,
bound up, greased, hardened, softened, wrapped
up, poured out medicines; and I know not what
other things they did not. Meanwhile, the patients
none the less perished under their hands, many
railing at them, and saying that it was either
through their ignorance or their carelessness that
they had come to ruin. I saw generally that
though their science awarded these good healers

some gain, it also constrained them (if they wished
to fulfil their duties) to much—indeed, very much
—hard and, in some cases, also disgusting work,
and that it brought them as much disfavour as
favour; and this pleased me not.

CHAPTER XV

THE PILGRIM BEHOLDS JURISPRUDENCE

(*Finis Juris.*)

THEN they again lead me to a spacious lecture-room, in which I saw more notable men than elsewhere. All along the walls they had painted masonry blockhouses, fences, ramparts, rails, partition-walls, and partitions; and through these, again, there were gaps and holes, doors and gates, bolts and locks, and together with them divers keys, hinges, and hooks. All these men in the lecture-room pointed to this, and attempted to measure where and how it would be possible to enter or not. And I asked: "What, then, are these folks doing?" The answer was that they were striving to discover how every man in the world could retain possession of his goods, and also transfer peacefully to himself the goods of others while maintaining order and concord. Then I said: "This is a pretty thing;" yet after watching it for some time, it disgusted me.

(*Jus Circa quid Versetur.*)

2. And this was mainly because they had enclosed within these barriers not the spirit or the

mind or the body of man, but only his worldly goods, a non-essential matter which seemed not to me worthy of the very hard toil that was, as I saw, bestowed on it.

(*Fundamentum Juris.   Perplexitas Juris.*)

3. Besides, I saw that all this science was founded only on the arbitrament of a few, so that if this man or that thought well to maintain that this thing or that was true, the others judged it accordingly ; or (I noted this here) according to the fashion in which a man's brain whirled, he built up or destroyed these fences and gaps.   Therefore there were many things here that were verily contrary to each other, and others had to break their heads in a wondrous subtle fashion to settle and arrange these differences ; at last I wondered that they should grow so heated and sweat so over petty matters, some of which hardly occurred once in a thousand years, and this with no little arrogance. For the better a man was able to burst through a gap and then again to stop it up, the more was he pleased with himself, and the more did the others praise him.   But some (wishing to show their wit also) opposed the others, and loudly declared that thus, and not otherwise, things must be enclosed and gaps filled up ;[1] then there were quarrels and disputes ; then they stepped apart, and one drew one design, another a different one, while all endeavoured to attract the onlookers.   When I had

[1] *I.e.*, the law expounded.

L

sufficiently viewed this fooling, I shook my head. " Let us hurry hence, for already am I afeard," I said. And the interpreter to me, with wrath: " Will nothing then please thee in this world? Even in the most noble things, man of an unstable mind, thou findest somewhat to blame." Impudence answered him: " His mind, meseems, sickens with religiousness. Let us lead him elsewhere; there perhaps will he find attraction."

CHAPTER XVI

THE PILGRIM WITNESSES THE PROMOTION OF MASTERS AND DOCTORS

AND lo! the sound of a trumpet, as if they were summoning men to a festival; and Searchall, knowing what would happen, says: "Well, let us yet turn back; here there will be somewhat to behold." "What, then, will happen?" quoth I. He answered: "The academy will now crown those who, having been more diligent than the others, have attained the summit of science." "These," say I, "will now be crowned as an example to the others." Now being desirous of seeing so strange a thing, and seeing that crowds were already flocking together, I also enter behind them ; and behold, under a philosophical heaven, stood one with a paper sceptre, and some out of the crowd stepped up to him, demanding a testimony of their profound learning. He favoured their demand, saying that it was a seemly one, and ordered that they should explain in writing what they had learned, and what testimonial they required. Then one brought forth a summary of philosophy, another one of medicine, another one of jurisprudence; and their pouches, to make matters smoother, abstained not from bribery.

2. The man then led them forward, one by one, and pasted on their foreheads the words: "This is a master of the free arts; this a doctor of medicine; this a licentiate of both laws,"[1] and so forth; and he confirmed all this with his seal, ordering all present and not present, at the risk of the wrath of the goddess Pallas, not to address them otherwise than by this title when they met them. And then he dismissed them and the whole crowd. Then I said: "Will, then, nothing more happen?" "And is this, then, not sufficient for thee?" the interpreter said. "Dost thou not see how all give way to these men that have been crowned?" And freely the others made way for them.

3. But none the less, I, who ever wished to see what would then happen to these men, watched one of these masters of arts; then they asked him to count something together, but he knew not how to do so; they then told him to measure something, he knew not how to do so. They asked him to name the stars, he knew not how to do it; they asked him how to expound syllogisms, he knew not how to do it; they asked him to talk in strange tongues, he knew not how to do it; they asked him to speak in his own language, he knew not how to do it; at last they asked him to read and write, he knew not how to do it. "But what a sin is this," I said, "to call yourself a master of the seven arts, and then to know not one?" The interpreter answered: "If

[1] *I.e.*, civil and ecclesiastical law.

one learneth not, a second, a third, a fourth does; all cannot be perfect." "Now I understand," I said, "that after spending a lifetime in the schools, after laying out a fortune on this, after having received titles and seals, it is at the end still necessary to inquire whether a man has learnt something. God help me against such mismanagement." "Thou wilt not cease thy sophistry," said he, "till thou hast come to grief; continue then to prattle pertly, but I swear that thou wilt encounter some evil." "Well, then," quoth I, "be it that they are masters and doctors of seven times seventy sciences; be it that they know all things or none, I will say naught more. Only let us go hence."

CHAPTER XVII

THE PILGRIM BEHOLDS THE ESTATE OF PRIESTHOOD

(*The Pagans.*)

AND they lead me through certain passages, and we come to a market-place in which stood a multitude of churches and chapels built in divers shapes, and crowds were entering them, and then again leaving them; and we step into the one that was nearest, and behold, there were in every direction engravings and casts of men and women, also of divers animals, birds, reptiles, trees and plants; everything also was full of pictures of the sun, the moon, and the stars, and even of most vexatious devils. Now of those who entered, each one chose what pleased him, knelt before it, kissed it, incensed it, and sacrificed to it. But what appeared to me wondrous was the concord among these men; for though each one indeed performed his devotion differently, they yet permitted this, and peacefully allowed each one to retain his opinion (a thing that I saw not afterwards elsewhere). But then a certain stinking smell overcame me, so that terror seized me, and I hurried forth.

(The Jews.   Talmudi Figmenta.)

2. We then enter into another temple, white and
clean, in which there were but images of living
beings ; some of these were shaking their heads,
muttering somewhat in a low voice ; others raised
themselves, stopped their ears and then opened
their mouths wide, emitting a sound not dissimilar
from the howl of a wolf. Then they crowded
together and looked at certain books ; and stepping
up to them I saw wondrous paintings ; for instance,
a feathered and winged beast, birds also without
feathers and wings, beasts with the limbs of men,
and men with the limbs of beasts, one body with
many heads, and then again a head with many
bodies. Some of these monsters had instead of a
head a tail, others again a tail instead of a head ;
others had eyes under their belly, and feet at their
backs ; some, again, had countless eyes, ears, feet ;
others had nothing of this sort ; and all this was
strangely displaced, twisted, bent, crooked, and
most unequal. For one limb was a span, another
fathoms long ; one had the breadth of a finger,
another that of a barrel ; generally everything was
monstrous, more than can be believed. They,
however, said that these were but vain tales, and,
praising how fine it was, the elders expounded the
mystery to the younger men. And I said : " Who,
then, could believe there were men who could relish
such tasteless things ? Let us leave them ; let us
go elsewhere." And going out, I see that these

men walked about among the others, but displeased all, and caused but laughter and scorn. This induced me also to contemn them.

(*The Mahomedans.*)

3. We then enter another temple, which was rounded, and no less pretty than that of the others; but it was without ornaments, except a few letters on the walls and carpets on the floor. Meanwhile, the people within demeaned themselves quietly and piously; they were clothed in white, and were great lovers of cleanliness, for they were ever bathing; also did they give alms to the poor, so that in consequence of their behaviour I felt some affection for them. And I said: "What motive, then, have these men for their actions?" Searchall answered: "They carry under their clothing." And then I step nearer and endeavour to see. But they said that this was fitting but for the interpreters. Still, I wished to see, and based my request on the permission that I had received from the lord Fate.

(*A Summary of the "Al Koran."*)

4. And a tablet was procured and shown me, on which stood a tree with its roots extending upward towards the sky; but its branches jutted into the earth. All around a large number of moles were digging, and one large mole went round, called the others together and directed their work. And they told me that manifold delicious fruits grew on the

branches of this tree under the earth, which, they said, these quiet and industrious little animals obtained. "And this," quoth Searchall, "is the summary of this their religion." And I understood that its foundation was on the air of vain opinion, and that its purpose and fruits was but to burrow in the earth, to seek solace in invisible delights that existed not, and blindly to search for they knew not what.

(*Mahomedanism is founded on Force.*)

5. And leaving this spot, I said unto my guide: "How, then, do these men prove that this is a certain and true foundation of a religion?" He answered me: "Come and see." And we go behind the church to a market-place, and behold these white-clothed and well-washed men ran about with tucked-up sleeves, with sparkling eyes, biting their lips, roaring fiercely, sabring all they met, and wallowing in human blood. Then I was afeard, ran back, and said: "What, then, are these men doing?" The answer was: "They are discussing concerning religion, and proving that the 'Al Koran' is a true book."

(*There is Discord between the Persians and the Turks concerning the " Al Koran."*)

6. And we again enter the temple, and lo! among those also who carried the tablet there was, as I ascertained, strife as to which was the foremost mole.

Some, indeed, that one alone ruled the smaller moles, others that he should have two assistants; and on this matter they quarrelled among themselves, as they had with those outside the temple, and they disputed by means of iron and fire till it was terrible to behold.

CHAPTER XVIII

THE PILGRIM BEHOLDS THE CHRISTIAN RELIGION

AND seeing that I was terrified, my guide said: "Now let us go forth, and I will show thee the Christian religion, which, founded as it is on the certain revelations of God, satisfies both the simplest and the wisest; just as it brings heavenly truth clearly to the light, so also it defeats hostile errors, and it glories in concord and love. In the midst of countless adversities, it has remained unconquered, and will continue so. From this wilt thou readily be able to understand that the origin of this religion must proceed from God, and that here thou canst obtain true solace." And I rejoiced over this speech, and we went further.

(*Baptism.*)

2. And when we arrive, I see that they had a gate through which all had to pass. The gate stood in the water, and each one had to ford it, to wash himself, and assume the badge of these men, which was of white and red colour, and to swear that he would stand by their rights and rules, believe as they did, pray as they did, observe the same

commands as they did. And this pleased me as somewhat of a beginning of a noble order of things.

3. When I had passed through the portal, I see large crowds of men, and some of them different from the others by the vestments that they wore. These stood apart in a recess, and showed the people what appeared an image, painted so daintily that the more a man gazed at it, the more he found in it to admire; but as it was adorned neither with gold nor with glittering colours, it was not very visible from a distance. Therefore I saw that those who stood at a distance were not so much charmed by its beauty, but that those who were nearer were never satiated beholding it.

(*The Image of Christ.*)

4. Those, then, who carried this image praised it exceedingly, calling it the Son of God, and saying that in it all virtues were pictured, and that it had been sent from heaven to earth that men might find in it an example of how they should practise virtue among themselves. And there was gladness and rejoicing; falling on their knees, they lifted their hands heavenward and praised God. And seeing this, I added my voice to theirs, and praised God that He had allowed me to arrive at this spot.

(*The Spiritual Feasts of the Christians.*)

5. Meanwhile, I hear many and divers admonitions that everyone should conform to this image,

and I see that they meet together at various places, and that those to whom the image was entrusted, make small counterfeits of it, and distribute them to all, as it were, in a covering, and they with piety take them into their mouths. Then I ask: "What are they doing here?" The answer was that it sufficed not merely to behold the often-named image outwardly, but that one must also enter into its innermost, so that a man could transform himself into its beauty. For all sins, they said, must vanish before this celestial medicine. And I, relying on this message, praised within myself the Christians as blessed men, who possessed among themselves such remedies and such help against evil.

(*Dissoluteness among the Christians.*)

6. Meanwhile, looking at some of those who had recently—as they said—received God, gave themselves up one after the other to drunkenness, quarrelling, impurity, thieving, and robbing. But I, trusting not mine eyes, gaze yet more carefully, and I see in truest truth that they drink and vomit, quarrel and fight, rob and pillage one another both by cunning and by violence, neigh and skip from wantonness, shout and whistle, commit fornication and adultery worse than any of the others I had seen; briefly, everything they did was in contradiction to the admonitions they had received and to their own promises. Therefore was I troubled, and mournfully I said: "But

what, in the name of the Lord God, are they doing here?" Here I sought something different. "Wonder not so much," answered the interpreter. "That which is set forth to all men as an example is the degree of perfection which earthly weakness cannot always attain ; those who lead the others are, indeed, more perfect, but the ordinary men, occupied with many concerns, cannot equal them." "Let us, then," I said, "go among these leaders, that I may behold them."

(*On the Barrenness of Preachers.*)

7. And my guide then led me to those who stood on the steps ; and these, indeed, exhorted the people to love the image, but, as it seemed to me, but feebly. For if one listened and obeyed, well and good ; if he did not do so, it was well also. Some clanked keys, saying they had the power to close on those who did not obey them the gate by which man reaches God ; but meanwhile they closed it on no man, or, at least, when they did so, they did it as it were in jest. Indeed, I saw that they dared not do this very daringly ; for if one attempted to speak somewhat sharply, they reviled him, saying that he preached against persons. Therefore some, daring not to do so by word of mouth, in writing raged against sin ; but they screamed against these also, saying that they spread lampoons. Therefore, they either turned away from these men or threw them down the steps, replacing them by other more moderate

men. Seeing this, I said: "This is folly that, as
their leaders and councillors, they wish to have
followers and flatterers." "That is the way of the
world," said the interpreter, "and it harms not.
If these criers were given entire freedom, who
knows what they would not dare to do. A line
must be drawn for them beyond which they cannot
go."

(*The Carnality of Clerical People among the Christians.*)

8. "Let us, then," I said, "go to the spot where
they[1] are, so that I may see them alone, and discover how they manage their affairs outside of their
pulpits; there, at least, I know that no one measures
their steps or hinders them."   And we enter there
where priests only dwelt, and I, who think that I
shall find them praying and studying the mysteries
of religion, also found that some snored, wallowing
on feather-beds; others feasted, seated at divers
tables, cramming and pouring down things till they
became speechless; others performed dances and
leaps; others crammed with treasures pouches,
chests, and chambers; others pass their time in
love-making and wantonness; others employ themselves in fastening on spurs, daggers, swords, muskets; others bestirred themselves with dogs and
hares, so that they spent the least part of their time
with the Bible ; indeed, some hardly ever took it in
their hand, although they called themselves teachers

---

[1] *I.e.*, the priests.

of the Gospel.   Seeing this, I said: "Alas! oh my grief! these, then, are to be men's leaders heaven-ward and their models of virtue. Shall I then never find anything in this world that is free from fraud and deceit?" Hearing this, and understanding that I was complaining of their irregular life, some of those present looked askance [askew] at me, and began to mutter: "If I was seeking hypocrites and superficial devotees, I was to seek them elsewhere; they knew how to do their duty in church, and at home, and in the world to behave in a worldly fashion."   Then I was obliged to be silent, though I clearly saw that it is monstrous to wear a coat of mail over a surplice, a helmet over a barat, to hold the Word of God in one hand, a sword in the other; to carry Peter's keys in front and Judas's wallet behind; to have a mind educated by Scripture and a heart practised in fraud, a tongue full of piety and eyes full of wantonness.

(By Heavenly Gifts they help others, but not themselves.)

9. Then I see some especially who, in the pulpits, held forth in a very learned and pious fashion, and pleased themselves and others no less than if they had been angels; but their life was just as wild as that of the others, and I could not refrain from saying: "Lo! here are trumpets through which good things flow, but they themselves retain them not." The interpreter said: "This also is a gift of God, to speak prettily of divine matters." "It is

indeed a gift of God, but is it to stop at mere words?"

(Disorder among the Bishops.)

10. Meanwhile, seeing that all these men have over them their elders (called bishops, archbishops, abbots, provosts, deans, superintendents, inspectors, and so forth) weighty and worthy men, to whom all rendered much honour, and I thought: "Why, then, do not these restrain those of inferior rank?" And wishing to discover the cause of this I follow one of them into his chamber; then a second, a third, a fourth one, and so forth. And I find them all so busy that they had no time to watch the others. Except some things that they had in common with the others, they seemed to be occupied with counting their revenues and their church treasures (as they called them). And I said: "By mistake, I think, they call these men spiritual[1] fathers; they should be called fathers who receive revenue." The interpreter answered: "Yet care must be taken that the Church loseth not what God grants her, and what the pious forefathers have given her." Meanwhile, one stepped up to us who had two keys hanging from his girdle (he was called Peter), and he said: "Men and brethren, it is not seemly that, neglecting the Word of God, we should labour at desks and chests. Let us then

[1] This pun is untranslatable. In Bohemian, "spiritual" is "duchovni," while "duchodni" signifies a collector of rents or revenues.

M

choose men of good repute, and make over this work to them, while we ourselves are diligent at prayer and the service of the Word of God." And hearing this I rejoiced, for according to my mind this was good counsel. But hardly any agreed to this. They continued to add up accounts themselves, paid out and received money, while they either left prayer and the service of God's Word to others or performed these duties but hastily.

11. When one of them died and the cares of leadership had to be transferred to another, I saw much striving for favour, much searching and endeavouring to obtain patronage; each one struggled for a place before even the seat was cold. But he who had to confer it received judgments from them, and of them that differed greatly. One man claimed to be a kinsman; another a relation of the giver's wife; a third said that he had long served the elders and therefore hoped for a reward; a fourth, that he had a promise on which he relied; a fifth claimed to be placed in an honourable office because of his descent from honourable parents; the sixth brought forward the praise that he had obtained from others; the seventh offered gifts; the eighth, being a man of deep, high, and broad thoughts, claimed for himself a place where he could yet further enlarge his mind; and I know not what more. And seeing this, I said: "This assuredly is not beseeming, to thrust yourself forward for the purpose of obtaining such dignities; they should indeed wait till they are called." The interpreter answers: "Should then the unwilling ones be

called ? He who seeks dignities should make his
name known." " I verily believed," quoth I, "that
we must here await God's call." Then he again :
" Dost thou then think that God will call someone
from heaven ? God's call is the favour of the
elders, which everyone who prepares himself for
the calling is free to obtain." " I see, then," quoth
I, " that it is not necessary to seek for men, or
drive them into the service of the Church ; rather
to drive them from it ! Rather, if favour should
be sought at all, it should be sought therein, that
each man should by his humility, quietude, endear
himself to the Church, and not by such means as I
see here employed. Be it as it may, such things
are disorderly."

(The Christians' Trust in Faith without Works.)

12. Now, when my interpreter saw that I insisted
on this matter, he said to me : " It is true that
among Christians, even theologians, there is more
that is unbeseeming than elsewhere ; but this also
is true, that even Christians of evil life die well.
For the salvation of man dependeth not on deeds,
but on faith ; if this, then, is true, they cannot fail
to achieve salvation ; if but their faith is certain,
it is enough."

*(There are Disputes also concerning Faith.   The
Holy Gospel is the Touchstone.)*

13. " Do all, then, agree as to their faith ? " quoth
I. He answered : " There is indeed somewhat of

difference ; but all have the same foundation."
Then they lead me behind a railing into the centre
of a large church, where I behold a large, round
stone that hung downward by a chain. They
called it the touchstone. The foremost men
walked up to this stone, each one carrying somewhat in his hand, such things, for instance, as a
morsel of gold, silver, iron, lead or sand, chaff, or so
forth. Then each one touched the stone with that
which he had brought, and praised it, saying that
it had stood the test ; others who looked on said
that it had not done so. Then they wrangled
among themselves, for no one allowed his goods to
be defamed, nor would he approve of the goods of
another. They then reviled and cursed each other,
tearing and pulling each other's caps, ears, and
whatever part they could seize. Others wrangled
about the stone itself, and about its colour. Some
said that it was blue ; others that it was green ;
others that it was black. At last some were found
who said it was of changeable colour, and that
according to the thing that touched it, it appeared
differently. Some advised that the stone should
be broken up into bits ; when it had been pulver-
ised, then could one see its essence. Others allowed
not this. Others, going farther, said that this
stone caused but strife. It should be taken down
and removed ; then would they more easily com-
pose their differences. To this a large number,
even of the foremost, agreed. Others opposed this,
saying that they would rather lay down their
lives than allow it ; and indeed, when the strife

and the skirmishing increased, no few were killed, but the stone yet remained; for it was round and very slippery. He who stretched out his hand towards it could not grasp it, and it continued as before.

(The Christians are divided into Sects.)

14. Then going outside of this railing, lo! I see that this church had many little chapels, to which those went who had not been able to agree when before this touchstone, and behind each of them followed a number of men. They gave the people rules as to how they should differ from the others; some said that one should be marked by water or fire; others, that one should always have the sign ready at hand and in the pocket; others said that beside the principal image, at which all should gaze, men should, for greater perfection, carry with them also as many small ones as was possible; others said that when praying one should not kneel, for that was a thing of the Pharisees; others, again, said that they would not endure music among them, as it was a wanton thing; others, again, said that one should accept the teaching of no man, and be content with the innermost revelation of the spirit. When gazing at these chapels, I beheld somewhat wondrous regulations.

(Of these Chapels, one is the most wondrous.)

15. Now one of these chapels was the largest and finest, gleaming with gold and precious stones;

and in it was heard the sound of gay instruments. Into this one I was carefully led, and I was admonished to look around me, for here was a religious service more delightful than any other. And behold, along the walls there were everywhere images showing how a man could attain heaven. Here some were depicted who had made themselves ladders, set them heavenward and climbed up them ; others piled up hills and mountains one on the other, that they might rise ˈupward by such means; others fashioned for themselves wings and fastened them on ; others caught up some winged creatures, tied them together, attached themselves to them, hoping with them thus to fly upward, and so forth. There were also many priests of divers shape, who showed these images to the people and praised them ; at the same time, they taught them to distinguish themselves from the others by divers ceremonies. Now one clothed in gold and purple sat on a high throne distributing rare gifts to the followers and councillors who were his intimates. And it seemed to me that this was right orderly and more merry than anything else. But when I had visited the other sections, and saw that these attacked them, severely censured and blamed these things,[1] I became suspicious; particularly when I saw that they answered and defended themselves but timidly, while by means of stoning, water, fire and the sword, and on the other hand by means of gold, they enticed to them the misled people. Also did I behold among them much discord, disputes, hatred,

I.e., the ceremonies of the Roman Catholic Church.

striving to thrust others from their offices, and other disorders. Thence I went forth from here to behold those who are called reformed.

(*These others endeavour vainly to unite.*)

16. And I hear and see that some of these chapels (two or three that were near to each other) deliberated as to how they could become one ;[1] but they could find no compromise. Everyone maintained that which was in his own head, and endeavoured to persuade the others to agree to it. Some foolish ones took up at random any doctrine that came in their way ; others more cunningly entered or left the divers chapels according to what appeared to them advantageous ; and at last I was displeased by the confusion and wavering among these dear Christians.

(*The true Christians.*[2]   *The Pilgrim recognises them not.*)

17. Among these men there were some who said they had no concern with this strife ; they walked

[1] In Germany, and [in Bohemia up to the suppression of all Protestant sects, the Lutherans, Calvinists, and brethren of the Unity (Komensky's own church) frequently endeavoured to formulate a joint profession of faith. This attempt met with little success. In Bohemia such a profession, the "Confessio Bohemica," was actually drawn up. (*See* my "Bohemia an Historical Sketch," pp. 274-287, and elsewhere.)

[2] Komensky here gives under this name a perhaps slightly idealised description of the community to which he himself belonged ; he has dealt with the same *motif* somewhat

on silently, quietly, as in thought, looking heavenward, and bearing themselves affably towards all,
and they were insignificant and ragged, exhausted
by fasting and thirst ; but the others but laughed
at them, cried shame on them, hissed them,
scratched and toused them, pointed at them with
their fingers, tripped them up, and mocked them.
But they, enduring everything, went their way, as
if they had been blind, deaf, dumb.   Now when I
saw them come forth from behind the railing and
enter the choir, I wished to enter there also and see
what they had there.   But the interpreter pulled
me back.   "What dost thou wish to do there ?   Dost
thou desire to become a laughing-stock ?   That
were indeed a desirable thing ! "   So I entered not,
and, alas! I overlooked this spot, deceived by my
evil companion, Falsehood.   I missed here the
centre of heaven and earth, and the road leading to
the place where man is saturated with joy.   I was
again led into the turmoil of the labyrinth of the
world, till my God saved me and guided me back
again to the path which I had left at this spot.
What then befell,[1] and how it befell, I shall tell
later; but at the time I judged not thus, for

more extensively in the last chapters of this book.   As
so many passages in Komensky's masterpiece have an auto-
biographic character, it may be well to mention that he is
in this chapter referring to the imaginary "pilgrim."
Komensky himself belonged to the Unity during his
whole life.

[1] Komensky here refers to his mystical union with God,
which he describes in those chapters of his book, the last
ones, that are entitled the " Paradise of the Heart."

seeking but outward peace and comfort, I hastened away to gape at other things.

(An Accident befalls the Pilgrim while in the Estate of the Clergy.)

18. I will not pass over in silence what further befell me in this street. My friend Impudence had persuaded me to join the estate of the ecclesiastics, saying that it was my destiny to belong to it; and, indeed, I confess that this was according to my wishes, though not everything in that estate pleased me. And I allow myself to be inveigled; I assume cap and cowl, and step with others into divers side chapels till a separate one was allotted unto me. But looking back at those behind me, I see that one turned his back on me; another shook his head over me; a third winked with his eye at me evilly; a fourth threatened me with his fist; a fifth pointed at me with his finger. At last,[1] some rushing at me, push me away and put another in my place, threatening that they would do yet worse; and I was afeard and ran away, saying to my guides: "Oh, over this most wretched world,

[1] Though this is a mere conjecture, I think that, in distinction to the earlier part of this chapter, Komensky here writes autobiographically. Komensky's dissensions with members of his community were, indeed, later than the year 1623, in which he wrote the "Labyrinth." But it is known that the later editions, particularly that of Amsterdam, 1663, from which I translate, contains additions. A full commentary on the "Labyrinth" and thoroughly critical edition of the book have, unfortunately, not yet been published in Bohemia.

one thing after the other fails!" "No doubt," said the interpreter. "Why takest thou not heed not to incite men against thee? He who would be among men must accommodate himself to men, not behave like a fool, as thou always dost." "I know now naught but to abandon everything," I said. "Not so, not so," said Impudence; "we must not despair. If thou art not fit for this, thou wilt be fit for somewhat else. Come but on, and we will see other things," and taking me by the hand, he led me on.

CHAPTER XIX

THE PILGRIM BEHOLDS THE ORDER OF THE MAGISTRATES

(The divers Ranks of Magistrates.)

WE then enter another street, where on all sides I behold countless chairs, some higher and some lower. Now they called those who sat on them Sir Judge, Sir Burgomaster, Sir Official, Sir Regent, Sir Burgrave, Lord Chancellor, Lord-Lieutenant, Lord Justice, Gracious King, Prince, and so forth. And the interpreter said to me: " Now, thou hast before thee the men who deliver judgments and sentences in law-suits, punish the evil, defend the good, and maintain order in the world." " This is, indeed, a fine thing, and one that is necessary for mankind," quoth I. " But whence do they take these men ? " He answered me: " Some are born to this estate; some are elected to it either by these men or by the community because they are considered the wisest of all, the most experienced, and the men best informed of law and justice." " This also is well," quoth I.

1. But at that moment it was for a short time granted me to see clearly, and I behold that some obtain these seats by purchase, others by entreaty,

others by flattery, while others, again, occupied them
arbitrarily. Seeing this, I exclaimed : " Lo, what
disorder ! " " Hush, froward one," said the interpreter ; " thou wilt fare ill if they hear thee ! "
" Why, then," quoth I, " do not these men wait till
they are chosen ? " He answered : " Ha ! these
men are no doubt conscious that they are capable
of such work ; if the others admit them to it, what
concern is that of thine ? "

3. Then I am silent ; and after putting my
spectacles aright, I look at these men attentively
and witness an astounding sight—to wit, that hardly
one of them possessed all his limbs ; almost every
one of them was devoid of some necessary thing.
Some had not ears through which they could hear
the complaints of their subordinates ; some had not
eyes to see the disorder before them ; some had not
a nose to scent the plots of knaves against the
right ; some had not a tongue to speak in favour
of the dumb, oppressed ones ; some had no hand to
carry out the decrees of justice ; many also had not
a heart to do what justice requires.

4. But those who had all these things were woe-
ful men, as I saw ; for they were continually
importuned, so that they could neither eat quietly
nor sleep sufficiently, while the others spent more
than half their time in idleness. And I said :
" Why, then, do they entrust these judgments to
such men, who have not the members necessary for
the purpose ? " The interpreter answered that this
was not so, but that it only appeared thus to me
for he said : " ' Qui nescit simulare nescit regnare.'

He who would rule others must often not see, not
hear, not understand, even if he sees, hears, under-
stands. This, as thou art inexperienced in public
affairs, thou canst not understand." " Yet, on my
faith," quoth I, " I see that they have not the
members they should have." " And I," said he,
" counsel thee to be silent; indeed, I promise thee
that if thou ceasest not to cavil thou shalt find thyself in a place that will please thee not. Knowest
thou not that censuring judges endangers the neck ? "
Then I was silent and gazed quietly at everything.
But it does not seem to me fitting that I should
narrate all that I saw at the divers chairs. On two
things only will I touch.

(*Disorder and Injustice are frequent among Judges.*)

5. I observed most carefully the law-court of the
senators, and I saw that the names of the lord-
justices were as follows :—Judge Nogod, Judge
Lovestrife, Judge Hearsay, Judge Partial, Judge
Loveself, Judge Lovegold, Judge Takegift, Judge
Ignorant, Judge Knowlittle, Judge Hasty, Judge
Slovenly. The president of them all was Lord
Thus-I-will-it. From their names I immediately
began to perceive what manner of judges they
were ; but an example of it befell in my presence.
Simplicity was accused by an enemy of having
defamed some good men by calling them usurers,
misers, drunkards, gluttons, tipplers, and I know
not what else. As witnesses, Calumny, Lie, and
Suspicion were brought forward. As council,

Flattery appeared for one side, and Prattler for the other; but Simplicity declared that she needed him not. Questioned whether she admitted that of which she was accused, she said: "I admit, dear my lords. Here I stand; I cannot speak differently. May God help me!" Then the judges, crowding together, collected the votes. Nogod said: "It is, indeed, true what this wench sayeth; but what business had she to gossip thus? If we let it pass, she will use her jaw against us also. I give my vote in favour of her being punished." Lovestrife said: "Certainly; for if such a thing were passed over once, others also would ask for forbearance." Hearsay said: "I do not, indeed, truly know what has happened, but as the complainant lays so much importance on this matter, I conclude that it really gives him pain. Let her then be punished." Partial said: "I had known before that this chatterer blabs out everything she knows. It is necessary to stop her jaws." Loveself said: "The injured man is my good friend. She should at least have spared him, for my sake, and not have affronted him in this fashion. She deserves punishment." Lovegold said: "You know how bounteous he [1] has proved himself; he deserves our protection." Takegift said: "It is so; we would be ungrateful if we did not attend to his complaint." Ignorant said: "I know no precedent in this case. Let her suffer as she has deserved." Then Knowlittle: "I do not understand the case. I agree to whatever sentence you may pass." Slovenly said: "Be it as

[1] *I.e.,* the complainant.

it may. I accede to everything." Careless said :
" Can we not defer the lawsuit ? Perhaps the
matter will clear itself up later." Hasty said :
" Not so ; let us gladly pass judgment." Then
the Lord-Justice said : " Certainly ; whom have we
to consider ? As the law will sit, so must it be
done." And rising, he delivered his sentence :
" As this prattling woman has given herself up to
much unbecoming conduct, and shows ill-will to
good men, she shall receive forty stripes, save one,
to subdue her unbridled tongue, and as an example.
This sentence is to be made known to her." Then
the complainant, with his council and witnesses,
bowed and thanked for this just finding. It was
made known to Simplicity also. But she gave
herself up to crying and to wringing of hands.
Then saying that she had not respected the law,
they ordered her punishment to be rendered yet
more severe, and she was seized and led forth to
punishment. Seeing the injustice that had been
done, I exclaimed, unable to contain myself : " Oh,
if all tribunals in the world are as this one, may
God the Almighty so help me that I may never be
a judge, or go to law with anyone ! " " Be silent,
madman," said the interpreter, and he placed his
fist before my mouth. " On my oath, I say that
through thy talking thou wilt receive as bad and
worse punishment than this woman." And, indeed,
lo ! the plaintiff and Flattery already begin to bring
forward witnesses against me. Then perceiving
this, and being afeard, I hurried thence, I know
not how, scarcely drawing breath.

(On the Perversity of Lawyers.)

6. While I then take breath outside these law-courts and wipe my eyes, I see many coming to the courts bringing plaints, and immediately the advocates (Prattler, Flattery, Guidewrong, Procrastination, and others), met them and offered their services, considering not so much what plaint as what purse each man had. Each man carried with him carefully his law-book (I think that I had not seen that among the theologians),[1] and sometimes looked at it. Now, on some of these books I saw inscriptions such as " The Devouring Torment of the Land," or " The Rapacious Defraudment of the Land." [2]   But unable to look at this any longer, I went away sighing.

(The unlimited Power of Princes and the Stratagems of their Officials.)

7. Then Searchall said to me: "The best yet remains.   Come and behold the rule of kings, princes, and others who reign over their subjects by hereditary right ; perhaps this will please thee." And we go to another place, and behold, men sat there on chairs that were so high and broad that it

[1] The Bohemian word "zákon," *i.e.* law, has also the significa-tion of " Bible " or " Testament."

[2] Komensky's words here are parodies on the names of ancient Bohemian law-books.   His puns are, unfortunately, untranslatable.

was rare that anyone could approach them and
reach them, except by means of strange instruments; for each one, instead of ears, had long tubes
on both sides, and those who wished to say something had to whisper into them. But they were
crooked and full of holes, and many words escaped
outward before they reached the head, and those
that reached it were mostly altered. I marked
this, because not all who spoke received an answer;
at times even when one clamoured loudly enough
the sound did not penetrate to the brain of the
ruler. Sometimes, again, an answer was given, but
it was not to the point. Similarly, instead of the
eyes and the tongue there were tubes, and, seen
through them, things often appeared different from
what they really were, and an answer was given
that differed from the intentions of the ruler himself. Understanding this, I said: "Why, then, do
they not put away these tubes and see, hear,
answer with their own eyes, ears, tongue, as plain
people do?" "Because of the preciousness of their
person and the dignity of their rank there must be
such delaying ceremonies; or dost thou think they
are peasants, whose eyes, ears, mouth, everyone
may approach?"

(*The Great must have Councillors, however
inconvenient they may be.*)

8. Meanwhile, I see some who walk round the
thrones; of these some whisper somewhat into the
ears of their master by means of these tubes; others

N

place vari-coloured spectacles before his eyes; others burn incense before his nose; others first put his feet closer together, and then again separate them; others adorn and strengthen his throne. Seeing this, I ask: "Who are these? and what do they?" The interpreter answered: "They are the privy councillors who instruct the kings and great lords." "I should not," quoth I, "allow this if I were in their position; rather should I wish to be able to use my own limbs and act as I wished." One man said: "He must not take everything on his shoulders; nor would he be permitted to do so!" Then said I: "These great lords are more wretched than peasants, being so bound that they cannot even move, except in accordance with the will of others." "Yet are they thus more certain in their own minds," quoth he; "but now look at these men!"

(*Without Councillors, Matters are yet worse.*)

9. And I look back, and behold some of those who sat on these chairs did not allow themselves to be thus molested, and drove these councillors from them; and this was according to my wishes. But here I immediately found other evils. In the place of the few that had been driven away, there came many others, and they tried to blow and whisper into the ears, nose, and mouth of the ruler; to close and disclose his eyes in divers fashions; to stretch out his hands and feet now in this, now in that direction; particularly also did each one endeavour

to lead and draw him to the spot where he himself stood. Thus the unhappy lord knew not what to do, to whom he should give way, whom he should restrain, nor how he could be a match for them all. And I said : " I see already that it is better to trust a few chosen ones than to be the prey of them all ; but could not all this be contrived somewhat differently ? " " And how could it be contrived ? " quoth he. " The estate of the ruler compels him to receive complaints, accusations, petitions, entreatments, arguments, and counter-arguments from all, and to grant justice to all. Let it then be according to the customs of these men."

(*Careless Lords.*)

10. Then the interpreter showed me some lords, who allowed nobody near them except men who strove and worked for the ruler's comfort. And I saw that they had around them men who were skipping round them, stroking them, placing pillows under them, and mirrors before their eyes, cooling them with fans, picking up the feathers and sweepings around them, kissing their garments and shoes ; yet all this was but deceit ; some even licked the spittle and snivel that came forth from their masters, praising it as being sweet. But all this, again, pleased me not ; particularly when I had seen that the throne of almost every one of these rulers frequently shook, and was, when he least expected it, overturned ; for he lacked those trusty supporters.

(*A Dangerous Adventure of the Pilgrim.*)

11. Now it befell that in my presence a royal throne suddenly shook,[1] broke into bits, and fell to the ground. Then I heard noise among the people, and looking round, I see that they were leading in another prince and seating him on the throne, while they joyously declared that things would now be different from what they had been before ; and everyone, rejoicing, supports and strengthens the new throne as much as he can. Now I, thinking it well to act for the common welfare (for thus they called it), came nearer and contributed [2] a nail or two to strengthen the new throne ; for this some praised me, while others looked askance at me. But meanwhile the other prince recovered himself, and he and his men attacked us with cudgels, thrashing the whole crowd, till they fled, and many even lost their necks. Maddened by fear I almost lost consciousness, till my friend Searchall, hearing that they were inquiring as to who had aided and abetted the other throne, nudged me that I also might flee. Falsehood said that it was not neces-

---

[1] Komensky here alludes to the temporary expulsion of the Austrians from Bohemia, the short reign of Frederick of the Palatinate, and the subsequent victory of Ferdinand II. of Austria.

[2] This allusion to aid given by Komensky to the cause of King Frederick is somewhat obscure, as he naturally did not refer to it in any of his writings. His sympathies were, of course, with the elector Palatine, and his father-in-law Cyrillus assisted the President of the Prague Consistory, Dicastus, at the coronation of King Frederick.

sary. While I then reflect which of them I shall
obey, I am struck by one of the cudgels which they
were brandishing near ; then I recovered consciousness, and I hastily fly into a corner. Thus did I
understand that to sit on these chairs, to be near
them, or indeed to touch them in any way, is
dangerous. Then I went forth from here most
gladly, and I resolved never again to return. And
thus spake I to my guides : " Let him, who will,
approach these heights. I shall not do so."

(There is Disorder everywhere among Men.)

12. And I was yet more certain of this when I
discovered that though these men wished to be
called the world-rulers, yet everything was full of
unruliness. For whether the prince permitted his
subjects to communicate with him through the
tubes, or whether he delivered his decrees by means
of the whispers of others, I saw as much evil as
justice ; I heard as much groaning and lamentation
as merriment ; I found that justice was inter-
meddled with injustice, and violence with legality.
I clearly understood that the town-halls, the law-
courts, the chanceries are as much the workshops
of falsehood as of righteousness, and that those who
call themselves the defenders of order in the world
are as much (and often more) the defenders of disorder than of order. And wondering how much
vanity and glittering misery is concealed within
this estate, I took leave of these men and went
away.

CHAPTER XX

THE ESTATE OF SOLDIERY

(*The Cruelty of Man.*)

WE then enter the last street, and on the first market-place I see no few men clothed in red ; approaching them, I hear that they are deliberating among themselves as to how they could give wings to Death, so that she could in a moment penetrate everywhere both near and far ; item, how that which had been built during many years could be destroyed in an hour. And I become afeard on hearing such speech, for hitherto, wherever I had looked at the deeds of men, the education and the increase of mankind, and the furthering of the comforts of human life, had alone been talked of and striven for. But these men deliberated on the destruction of the lives and of the comforts of men. Then the interpreter said : " The endeavours of these men also tend to that purpose, but by a somewhat different path—to wit, they remove that which is harmful. Later thou wilt understand this."

(Recruiting.)

2. Meanwhile we come to a gate, where, instead of gate-keepers, there stood some with drums, who asked each one who wished to enter whether he had a purse. Then when he showed and opened it, they put some silver into it, and said: "Let this hide be considered as paid for." Then they bid the man enter what appeared to be a vault, and afterwards again conducted him out, loaded with iron and fire-arms; then they ordered him to proceed farther into the market-place.

(The Arsenal, or Armoury.)

And now becoming desirous to see what was in this vault, I immediately enter it. And behold, there lay there on the ground an endless mass of cruel weapons that thousands of carts could not have transported. There were weapons for stabbing, chopping, cutting, pricking, hacking, stinging, cutting down, tearing, burning; there were altogether so many instruments destined to destroy life, fashioned out of iron, lead, wood, and stone, that terror befell me, and I exclaimed: "Against what wild beasts are they preparing all these things?" "Against men," the interpreter answered. "Against men!" quoth I. "Alas! I had thought it was against some mad animal, or wild, furious beasts. But, in the name of God, what cruelty this is that men should devise such terrible things against other men!" "Thou art too fastidious," he said, laughing.

(The Life of Soldiers is licentious.)

4. And going onward, we come to a market-place, where I see herds of these men who were clothed in iron, and had horns and claws, and were fettered together in troops. They were crouching before what seemed troughs and jugs, into which that which they were to eat and drink was strewn and poured out for them ; and they, one after the other, gobbled and lapped it up. And I said : "Are hogs, then, being here fattened for butchery? I see, indeed, the appearances of men, but swinish deeds." "That is no inconvenience for men of that estate," said the interpreter. Meanwhile, they· rise from these troughs, give themselves to frolics and dancing, skipping and shouting. And the interpreter further: "Well, dost thou see the delights of this life? About what need they be anxious? Is it not merry to be here?" "I shall await what will befall later," quoth I. But they now begin to pursue and harry every man whom they met, who was not of their own estate. Then, wallowing on the earth, they committed —— and every infamy, without any shame or fear of God. Then I blushed and said : "Assuredly they should not be allowed to do this." "They must be allowed," said the interpreter, "for this estate claims much liberty." They then sat down and began to gobble, and after they had crammed themselves with food and drink

till they were speechless, they stretched themselves out on the earth and snored. Then they were led into the market-place, where rain, snow, hail, frost, sleet, thirst, hunger, and every sort of filth rained on them. Then no few trembled, panted, tottered, perished, the food of all dogs and crows. Yet others heeded not, and continued to revel.

(Description of a Battle.)

5. Then suddenly the drums beat, the trumpet resounds; then behold, all rise up, seize daggers, cutlasses, bayonets, or whatever they have, and strike mercilessly at one another, till blood spurts out. They hack and hew at one another more savagely than the most savage animals. Then the cries increase in every direction; one could hear the tramping of horses, the clashing of armour, the clattering of swords, the growl of the artillery, the whistle of shots and bullets round our ears, the sound of trumpets, the crash of drums, the cries of those who urged on the soldiers, the shouting of the victors, the shrieking of the wounded and dying. An awful leaden hail-storm could be seen; dreadful fiery thunder and lightning could be heard; now this, now that man's arm, head, leg flew away; here one fell over the other, while everything swam in blood. "Almighty God," quoth I, "what is happening? Must the whole world perish?"

Hardly had I somewhat recovered consciousness than I fled this spot, I know not how, nor whither

I went. When I had somewhat recovered my breath, I said, though still trembling, to my guides: "Whither, then, have you led me?" The interpreter answered: "Oh, on thee, effeminate one! To let others feel your power, that is what makes a man of you." "What have they then done to each other?" I said. He answered: "The lords fell out, and then the matter had to be settled." "What! do these men then settle it?" quoth I. "Certainly," the interpreter answered, "by such means; for who could make great lords, kings, and kingdoms that have no judge above them agree? They must decide the differences between them by means of the sword. He who surpasses the other in the usage of iron and fire takes the first place." "Oh, barbarity! oh, beastliness!" quoth I. "Was there then no other way to reconcile them? Wild beasts should thus settle their differences, not men."

(Those who remain after the Battle.)

6. Meanwhile, I see that they lead and carry from the battlefield many whose hands, arms, head, nose had been cut off, whose bodies had been transpierced, whose skin was in tatters, and who were everywhere dabbled with blood. While I could, from pity, scarce look at these men, the interpreter said: "All this will be healed; a soldier must be hardy." "What, then," quoth I, "of those who lost their lives here?" He answered: "Their hides had already been paid for." "How this?" said I.

"Hast thou, then, not seen how many pleasant things were previously granted them?" "And what unpleasant things also had they to endure?" quoth I; "and even if only delights had previously been their lot, it is a wretched thing to give food to a man only that he may be forced to go to the shambles directly afterwards. It is an ugly estate in any case. I like it not! I like it not! Let us go hence."

CHAPTER XXI

THE ESTATE OF THE KNIGHTS

(Wherefore Nobility and Coats-of-Arms are given.)

" Look now," said the interpreter, "what honour he receives who demeans himself bravely, and fights his way through swords and spears, arrows and bullets." Then they lead me to what appeared a palace, and here I see one who sat under a baldachin, and called to him some of those who bore them bravely in fight. And many came carrying with them skulls, crossbones, ribs, fists that they had hewed off the bodies of their enemies, and pouches and purses that they had taken from them. They were praised for this, and he who sat under the baldachin gave them a painted thing,[1] and peculiar liberties above the others. They carried these things on poles, so that all could see them.

(Others also crowd into this Estate.)

2. Seeing this, many, not only warriors as in the olden days, but others also who busied themselves

I.e., coats-of-arms.

with trade or book came forward, and unable to
show wounds and goods taken from the enemy, as
the others did, they drew out and presented their
own purses, or writings which had been up into
books.   And to them also such things were given
as to the others—indeed, frequently more gorgeous
ones ; and then they were admitted into a higher
hall.

(*The Splendour of Knights.*)

3. Entering behind them, I see bands of them
who were walking together ; they had feathers on
their heads, spurs on their heels, and steel around
their hips.   I did not approach them closely, and I
did well so.   For I soon saw that others who
meddled with them fared not well; for those
who approached them too closely, who did not
sufficiently make room for them, who did not bend
their knees to them sufficiently, who knew not how
to pronounce their titles sufficiently correctly, these
they struck with their fists.   Fearing that this
would befall me also, I begged that we might go
thence.   But Searchall said: "First look better at
them, but be careful."

(*Knightly Deeds.*)

4. So I look from a distance and behold their
deeds.   Then I see that their work (as they said
because of the privileges of their estate) consisted
in treading the pavement, sitting astride on the

back of a horse, hunting greyhounds, hares and wolves, driving the serfs to soccage,[1] placing them in towers,[2] and then again letting them out, sitting at long tables laden with divers dishes, and keeping their feet under them as long as possible, bowing daintily and kissing hands, playing skilfully at draughts or dice, prattling without shame of all obscene and lewd matters, and other such things. It was, they said, assured to them by their privileges that all they did should be called noble, and no one who was not a man of honour should assort with them. Some also measured each other's shields,[3] comparing the one with the other; and the greater and the more antiquated a man's shield was, the more was he esteemed. But if a man bore a new one, the others shook their heads over him. I saw much more there that appeared to me wondrous and absurd, but I may not tell everything. This only will I say, that after looking sufficiently at the vanities of these men, I again begged my guides to proceed elsewhere, and I obtained their consent.

(The Road to the Castle of Fortune.)

5. While we proceed, the interpreter says to me: " Well, now, thou hast beheld the labour and striving of men, and nothing has pleased thee; perhaps

[1] In Bohemian, "robota," the enforced labour which the Bohemian lords demanded of their serfs.

[2] *I.e.*, prisons.

[3] *I.e.*, coats-of-arms.

because thou hast thought that these men have naught but labour. Learn then now, that all these labours are the way that leads to that rest to which all who shirked not toil at last attain ; for when they obtain estates and wealth, or glory and honour, or comfort and pleasure, their minds have sufficient cause to rejoice. Therefore, then, will we now guide thee to this delightful castle, that thou mayest see what is the purpose of the labours of men." And I rejoiced at this, hoping to find there rest of the mind and consolation.

CHAPTER XXII

THE PILGRIM FINDS HIMSELF AMONG THE NEWSMEN

WHEN we drew near to the gate, I see a multitude of men in the market-place to the left, and Impudence says: "Lo! these also we must not omit." "What have they there?" quoth I. He answered: "Come and see." And we walk among them, and, behold, they stood there, two or three together; and one pointed with his finger at the other, averted his head, clapped his hands, scratched himself behind his ears. Finally some skip for joy; others cry. "What, then," quoth I, "are these men doing here? Are they acting a play of some fashion?" "Thou must by no means take such things for a play," said the interpreter; "they have real things before them, which, according to the manner in which they are fashioned, produce within them wonder, laughter, ire." "Yet would I gladly know what these things are at which they wonder, at which they laugh, and which cause their ire." Then gazing attentively, I behold that they were busying themselves with strange whistles, and that one man, bending towards the other, whistled somewhat into his ear; and when this piping was pleasing they rejoiced, and when it was doleful they were sad.

(*These Whistles have divers Sounds.*)

2. This also seemed wondrous, that the same whistles pleased some vastly that they refrained not from skipping for joy; to others the same sound appeared so grievous that they held their ears and ran away into corners, or they listened and then began to lament and cry bitterly. And I said: "This is a monstrous thing, that one and the same whistle should sound so sweet to some, and so bitter to others." The interpreter said: "It is the difference not of the sound, but of the hearing, that causes this. As one and the same medicine acts differently on patients according to their sickness, so also according to a man's inward passion and inclination to a thing the exterior sound of it appears either sweet or bitter."

(*The Limping Messenger.*)

3. "And where do they find these whistles?" "They bring them from everywhere," he said. "Seest thou not the vendors?" Then I look, and see that some walked and rode out who were appointed to carry about these whistles. Many of these rode forth on speedy horses, and many bought of them; others went on foot, and some even limped along on crutches, and prudent men bought rather from these, believing them to be trustworthy.[1]

[1] The "limping messenger" was a proverbial expression signifying "later news." At that period when communications were uncertain and difficult, the later news often contradicted that which had been first reported.

(The Delight of News-letters.)

4. Not only did I look at them, but I also listened myself, stopping at divers spots; and I understood that there was truly some pleasure in hearing the divers sounds that proceeded from various directions. But it pleased me not that some acted in an immoderate fashion, for they bought up all the whistles that they could obtain; then after having used them for a short time, they again threw them away. There were also men of divers estates who sat but rarely at home, and were ever on the watch in the market-place, ever giving their ears to that which was piped there.

(The Vanity of News-writing.)

5. Yet all this pleased me not when I saw the vanity of the thing; for sometimes a doleful note resounded, so that all grieved; then after a while a different sound was heard, and the terror turned to laughter. Some notes clang so sweetly that all rejoiced and exulted; but there soon came a change. The sound either ceased or turned to a mournful rattle; thus those who were guided by it often rejoiced and grieved over many things vainly, and it was but smoke.[1] It was therefore a cause of laughter that men allowed themselves to be deceived by every gust of wind. Therefore I praised those who, heeding not such folly, looked only to their work.

---

[1] *I.e.*, mystification.

*(There is Discomfort both with and without
News-letters.)*

6. But then, again, I beheld discomfort also among those who heeded not that which was piped around them. From every direction many things fell on their necks.[1] At last I see here this also that it was not safe for all to use these whistles. For as these sounds appeared different to different ears, disputes and scuffles arose therefrom ; and I myself met with an accident.[2] Having found a sharp-sounding whistle, I gave it to a friend ; then others seizing it threw it to the ground and stamped on it. Then they threatened me for having divulged such things, and seeing how furious and inflamed they were, I was obliged to flee. But as my guides ever solaced me with the thought of the Castle of Fortune, we went on towards it.

[1] *I.e.*, they were accused of various things.

[2] It is very probable that this is an allusion to some adventure of the author, of which otherwise nothing is known. He appears to have been accused of divulging secret news. It was not in the nature of a man such as Komensky to be always cautious.

CHAPTER XXIII

THE PILGRIM BEHOLDS THE CASTLE OF FORTUNE, AND FIRSTLY THE ENTRANCE TO IT

(Virtue is now but a Ruined Gate to Fame.)

Now when we approach this our dear castle, I first see crowds of men who were streaming thitherward from all the streets of the town; they walked round, endeavouring to spy out how they could reach the summit. Now to that castle only one lofty narrow gate led, but it had fallen into ruins, was covered up with earth, and overgrown with thorns. It was, meseems, called Virtue. Concerning it I was told that in olden times it had been built as the sole entrance to the castle, but that through some accident it had soon afterwards been covered up with earth; therefore some other smaller gates had been made, while this one was abandoned as being inaccessible and too difficult to enter.

(The Side Entrances.)

2. They therefore broke through the walls and made small gates at both sides, and looking at them I see on them inscriptions such as Hypocrisy, Lie,

Flattery, Vice, Cunning, Violence, and so forth. But when I called the gates by these names, those who were entering heard me; then were they incensed against me, grumbled, and wanted to throw me down, so that I had to keep my mouth closed. Then looking again, I saw that some still attempted to climb upward by the ancient gate through ruins and thorns. Some succeeded; others did not, and these returned to the side entrances, that were lower, and passed through them.

(Fortuna raises up those on whom by chance she seizes.)

3. Now I enter and see that this was not yet the castle, but that here also there was a marketplace, in which stood a crowd of people, who were looking anxiously at the palaces above them, and heaving sighs. When I asked what they were doing there, I was told that these were men who claimed to be admitted to the abode of the gracious Lady Fortuna, and who were waiting for a glance from her and for admission to her castle. "And are they not all to reach it? Surely all have striven bravely for that purpose!" The interpreter answered: "Each one may strive to the best of his power and knowledge; but in the end it depends on the Lady Fortuna, whom she wishes to receive and whom not. Thou mayest indeed wonder at the fashion in which it is done." Then I see that beyond the spot where I was standing there were no longer either gates or steps, but only a wheel,

that incessantly turned round and round; he who clung to it was lifted upward to a higher floor, here only received by the Lady Fortuna, and then permitted to proceed farther. But of those below, not everyone who wished to seize the wheel was allowed to do so; indeed, they only whom a functionary of Fortuna, named Chance, led to the wheel or placed on it; all others slipped. Now this administrator, Chance, walked in the midst of the crowd, and whom fortuitously she encountered, him she seized and placed on the wheel: even although some thrust themselves before her eyes, stretched out their hands and entreated her, alleging the hardships they had undergone: their sweat, weals, slashes, and other proofs of their toil. But I affirm that she must have been entirely deaf and blind,[1] for neither did she consider any person nor heed anyone's entreaties.

(*The Evil Case of those who seek Felicity.*)

4. There were many there of divers estate who, I knew, had grudged nor labour, nor sweat, both in fulfilling their duties and in endeavouring to pass through the gate of Virtue, or, indeed, through the side entrance also; yet could they obtain felicity? Another who thought not of such matters was taken by the hand and lifted upward. But of

---

[1] Comp. " Verum quam significationem habet ista mulier, quæ opinionem facit quod cæca sit ac mente capta ? Insistit autem lapidi rotundo," Hæc, " respondit Fortuna est. Nec cæca tantummodo est, sed surda etiam."—" Tabula Cebetis."

those who were waiting here, many greatly grieved that their turn never came, and some even became grey-haired.   Some, abandoning all hope of happiness, returned to their toilsome labours; then some of these were again seized with the same longing, again climbed upwards towards the castle, turning their eyes and hands in the direction of the Lady Fortuna.   Thus I learnt that the fate of these disappointed ones was in all cases wretched and doleful.

CHAPTER XXIV

(The Pilgrim beholds the Ways of the Wealthy.)

THEN I said to my guide : "Now would I gladly
see what there is on high, and how the Lady
Fortuna honours her guests." "It is well," said he,
and before I knew it we soared upward to where
the Lady Fortuna, standing on a globe, distributed
crowns, sceptres, commands, chains, buckles, purses,
titles and names, honey and sweetmeats ; and she
then only allowed them to proceed upward. Now
looking at the construction of the castle, which
consisted of three floors, I see that they conduct
some to the lower, others to the middle, others
again to the upper dwellings. Then the interpreter
said to me : "Here, in the lowest chambers, dwell
those whom the Lady Fortuna hath endowed with
gold and with goods; in the middle chambers dwell
those whom she feeds with pleasure; in the highest
palaces those reside whom she invests with glory,
that they may be observed, praised, honoured by
the others. Thou seest what a happy thing it is
for a man to succeed in coming here."

(The Fetters and Burdens of Wealth.)

2. "Let us then, by all means, go first among these
men," quoth I. Then we enter the lower chambers,

and behold, there was darkness there and gloom ; indeed, at first I saw scarcely anything, and heard but some clinking; and the stink of mould proceeding from all directions overcame me.   Then when I somewhat recovered my eyesight, I see that the chamber was full of people of all ranks, who walked, stood, sat, reclined, and each man's feet were loaded with fetters, and his hands bound with chains; some had also beside this a chain round their neck, and on their back a burden of some sort.   And I was afeard, and I said : " On my faith, have we then come to some prison-house ? " The interpreter answered, laughing : " What folly ! These are the gifts of the Lady Fortuna, with which she endows her beloved sons."   And looking first at one, then a second, then a third of these gifts, I see steely fetters, iron chains, and leaden or earthen crates.   " What strange gifts are these ! " quoth I.   " I should not desire them ! "   " But, oh fool ! thou seest not rightly," said the interpreter ; " for all this is sheer gold."   And I look again yet more carefully, and tell him that I none the less see there but iron and clay.   " Cavil not too much," he answered, " believe others rather then thyself ; see how the others value these things."

(*How the Rich are deceived.*)

3. And I look, and see to my surprise how these men delighted in being thus fettered ; this one counted the rings of his chain ; another took them

asunder, and then again collected them ; another
weighed his chain in his hand ; another measured
it by the span ; another took it to his mouth and
kissed it; another covered it with a kerchief to preserve it against frost, heat, and injury.   Sometimes
two or three met together, measured their chains,
'and weighed them one against the other.   He who
found his chain the lighter one grieved and envied
his neighbour.   He who had a larger and heavier
one strutted about, puffing himself up, boasting and
talking vaingloriously.   Yet some, again, sat quietly
in corners, rejoicing secretly only over their chains
and fetters ; for they wished not that others
should know of them, fearing, methought, enmity
and thievery.   Others, again, had trunks full of
clods and stones, which they carried with them
from place to place.   Others did not even put their
trust in such trunks; they fastened and hung so
many precious goods around their person that they
could neither stand nor walk, but merely crept
along gasping and panting.   Then seeing this, I
said: "Are these, then, in the name of all the saints,
to be called happy ?   Even when I beheld the labour
and striving of men, I saw nothing more wretched
than this happiness!"   Searchall said: "It is true
(why should I conceal it?) that merely to possess
Fortuna's gifts, and not to use them, gives more
anxiety than pleasure."   "But this is not the fault
of the Lady Fortuna," quoth the interpreter, "that
some know not how to use her gifts.   She is not
chary of her goods, but some misers know not how

to employ them either for their benefit or for that of others. Lastly, be it as it may, it is great happiness to possess riches." "I desire not such happiness as I see here," I said.

CHAPTER XXV

THE WAYS OF THE VOLUPTUOUS IN THE WORLD

(*Effeminate Voluptuaries.*)

SEARCHALL said : "Let us then go upward ; there wilt thou behold other things, delights only." And we mount the steps and enter the first hall ; and behold, there were here rows of couches that were suspended in the air, and rocked to and fro ; and they were bestrewed with soft cushions. Now on these couches some men wallowed who had around them a large crowd of servants, ready to render them all services, and carrying fly-flaps, fans, and other implements. If one of these men arose, hands were stretched out from all directions to assist him ; if he robed himself, soft silken garments only were handed to him ; if he had to go somewhere, he was carried on a chair bestrewed with pillows.[1] "Well, here hast thou that comfort which thou hast sought," said the interpreter. "What more canst thou desire ? To have so many good things that you need not heed anything ; to put your hand to no labour ; to have a plenitude of

[1] *I.e.*, a litter.

all things for which the mind craves; and to be not
even touched by a breath of cold or evil air, is not
that a blessed state?" I answered: "There is indeed
more merriness here than in those torture-chambers
below; but here, also, not everything pleaseth me."
"Of what dost thou again complain?" quoth he. I
said: "I see these idlers with prominent eyes
bloated faces, swollen bellies and limbs, that cannot
be touched, and seem full of sores. If someone
knocks or rubs against one of them, or an evil
wind blows, incontinently the man sickens. Often
have I heard that standing water rots and stinks,
but here I see instances of it. Thus these men
employ not their life; they sleep through it, and
they lounge[1] through it. This is naught for me."
"Thou art a wondrous philosopher," quoth the
interpreter.

(*Games and Plays.*)

2. Then they lead me to a second hall, where
everything appeared charming to the eyes and
ears. I behold delightful gardens, fishponds, and
parks, wild beasts, birds, fishes, sweet music of
divers sorts, and groups of merry companions who
skipped, ran after each other, danced, pursued
each other, fenced together, performed plays; and
I know not what else they did. "This, at least, is
not standing water," said the interpreter. "That

[1] If the word "to loaf" were a recognised one in the English
language, it would convey Komensky's meaning better than
any other.

is true; but let me look at these things." Then when I had looked, I said: "I see that no one is thoroughly satisfied [1] with these amusements; rather does each one soon become tired, and hurry elsewhere to seek enjoyment in something else. Therefore this seems to me but small delight." "If, then, thou seekest delight in food and drink, let us go there, where they can be found."

(*The Revellers.*)

3. Then we enter a third hall, and lo! I see the loaded tables and boards of the feasters, who had an abundance of all things before them, and made merry. Stepping near to them, I see how some continually cram and pour down food and drink, so that their bellies sufficed not; they had to loosen their belts. Others . . . . ; others picked out only dainty bits, smacking their lips, and wished that they had necks as long as that of a crane, so that they might enjoy the taste longer. Some boasted that for ten or twenty years they had never seen the sun either rise or set, because when it set they had never been sober any longer; and when it rose, they had never yet become sober again. They sat there, by no means mournfully, for divers music resounded, to which each man joined his own voice; thus songs, as of all birds and beasts, were heard: one howled, a second roared, a third crowed, a fourth barked, a

[1] Literally eats and drinks to sufficiency ("ne nají a ne napije"). This explains the interpreter's answer.

fifth chirped, a sixth twittered, a seventh croaked;
and so forth; and at the same time they made
strange grimaces.

(What Fare the Pilgrim had among the Feasters.)

4. And then the interpreter asked me how I
liked this harmony. "Not a bit," I said. Then
he said: "What, then, will please thee?   Art thou,
then, a log of wood, that not even this merriment
can enliven thee?"   Meanwhile, some of those who
sat round the tables see me; and one began to
drink my health, a second winked at me with his
eye, inviting me to sit down with them; a third
began to cross-question me as to who I was and
what I wanted; a fourth asked me, in a menacing
manner, why I did not say: "May God bless
you!"[1]   Then becoming incensed, I said: "What,
is God then to bless this swinish feasting?"   Then,
lo! before I had even finished my speech, plates,
dishes, goblets, and glasses begin to hail down upon
me; I was hardly able to escape them, and to
hurry forth hastily.   But it was easier for me, who
was sober, to flee, than for those drunkards to
strike me.   Then the interpreter said: "Well, did
I not say to thee long ago: 'Keep thy tongue
within thy teeth and cavil not.'   Strive to conduct
thyself according to man's way, and do not imagine
that others will heed thy noddle!"[2]

[1] It was customary in Bohemia to speak these words when
entering a room or when sitting down to table.

[2] *I.e.*, pay attention to thy ideas.

(The Pilgrim returns to the Hall.)

5. Impudence smiled, and taking me by the hand, " Let us go there again," he said ; but I would not. " Thou must, and canst yet behold these many things, if thou art but silent. Come, only act prudently, keeping somewhat aloof." And I allow myself to be persuaded, and enter again ; and—why should I deny it ?—I sat down among these men, allowed them to drink to me, and also pledged them, wishing at last to discover in what these delights consisted. I also began to sing and skip, and shout with the others ; in every way what they did, I did. Yet did I all this somewhat timidly, for it appeared to me that this was by no means fitting for me. Then some who saw that I did not excel in this laughed at me, while others were angered that I did not pledge them. But meanwhile, something under my coat begins to prick me, something under my cap stings me, something presses up my throat, my legs begin to stagger, my tongue rattles, and my head whirls round. I now become incensed against myself and my guides, and declare that this was conduct befitting not men, but beasts ; particularly after I had witnessed in others the voluptuousness of the voluptuaries.

(The Wretched Ways of Voluptuaries.)

6. Then I heard some complaining that they could neither relish food nor drink, nor bring them

down their throats; others pitied these men and, to help them, merchants had to hurry to all parts of the world in search of things that might be to the taste of these men; cooks had to examine samples of spices, that were to give the dainties a peculiar smell, colour, taste, and aid in conveying them into the stomachs of these; doctors had . . . Thus with much trouble and expense that which was to be poured and crammed into them[1] was sought out, and with much learning and cunning given unto them, causing them much pain in the stomach and elsewhere. And thus they constantly suffered of sickness . . . ; they slept badly, hemmed, sneezed, slobbered, and vomited; the tables and corners of the hall were full of divers filth; they walked and wallowed about with . . . , podagric feet, trembling hands, blear eyes, and so forth. "Are such things, then, to be considered pleasures?" quoth I. "Let us hence, that I may not say somewhat, and evil befall me there through." Then averting my eyes and stopping my nose, I went thence.

(*Veneris Regnum. Libidinis æstus Morb. . .*
Libido desperationis Præcipetium. . . .)

7.   .   .   .   .   .   .

---

[1] *I.e.*, medicines.

CHAPTER XXVI

THE WAYS OF THE GREAT OF THE WORLD

(*The Discomforts of the Great.*)

WE now enter the higher palace, that was quite open, having above it no covering but the firmament. And behold, there were here many seats, some of which were higher than the others; all were close to the verge that they might be seen from the city below. Men sat on them, some higher and some lower, according to the manner in which the Lady Fortuna had placed them. All passers-by gave them honour (though but ostensibly), bent their knees and bowed their heads. And the interpreter said to me: "Is it not a fine thing to be so exalted that you are seen from everywhere, and all have to gaze on you?" And I added: "And also to be so exposed that snow, rain, hail, heat, and cold strike at you." He answered: "What mattereth that? It is, indeed, a fine thing to be on such a spot, in which you attract the attention of all, and wherein all must notice you." "They do, indeed, watch them," quoth I; "but such watching is far more of a burden than of a comfort. That many watch for

226

these men, I already see; they may not and cannot move without all seeing them and passing judgment on them. What comfort is there in this?" I felt the more certain of this when I saw that if before them great respect was rendered to them, there was behind them and at their sides just as much disrespect. Then also behind each of those who was seated on his throne there stood some who looked asquint at him, muttered about him, and shook their heads over him, mocked him, soiled his back with spittle, snivel, and other matters; others, contriving his fall, undermined his throne, and in my presence this and other accidents befell full many.

(*The Dangers of the Great.*)

2. Now these seats, as I have said, stood on the verge; if one of them was pushed even very slightly, it was immediately overturned, and he who previously puffed himself up now fell downward.[1] The seats were so unstable that if anyone touched them they turned over, and he who sat there found himself on the ground. The higher a seat was, the easier it was to shake it. I found also much malice among these men. They looked at one another jealously; some drove others from their thrones, deprived them of their ruling powers, knocked off their crowns, blotted out their titles. Thus everything was ever chang-

---

[1] It has been impossible to render Komensky's pun on the words "douti" (to swell or puff) and " dolu " (downward).

ing; one climbed up to a throne,[1] another either crept down or fell down over heels. Beholding this, I said: "Oh, this is evil, that the reward of the long and hard toil that these men had to endure before they secured these seats should be so short! Indeed, before a man has begun to enjoy his honours they have already come to an end." The interpreter answered: "The Lady Fortuna must distribute her gifts in this fashion, that all whom she wishes to favour may receive their share; one must give way to the other.

[1] This passage is very characteristic of the period of the Thirty Years' War, and its sudden changes of Government. Thus Frederick of the Palatinate for a time took the place of Ferdinand of Austria as ruler of Bohemia; Wallenstein became Duke of Mecklenburg; Bernhard of Weimar attempted to establish his sovereignty on the banks of the Upper Rhine.

CHAPTER XXVII

(Fama ferme vulgi Opinione constat.)

"Besides," the interpreter further said, "the Lady Fortuna can also honour by immortality those who bear themselves well in the world, or whose merits deserve such a reward." "How, then, is this?" quoth I. "That is, indeed, a glorious thing to become immortal! Show it me, then." And Searchall bids me turn round, and shows me a yet higher hall or balcony that projected to westward from the palace; it was also uncovered, and from the lower hall steps led up to it. At the foot of the steps there was a small door, at which sat one who had eyes and ears all over his body, so that it was monstrous (they called him Censuram vulgi, Judgeall). To him each one who wished to enter the hall of glory had to declare his name, and also to show all the things through which he hoped to be worthy of immortality, and hand them over for examination. Now, when in the man's deeds there was something singular and unusual, be it good or bad, they allowed him to go upward; if not, he was left below. Now, those that arrived at that gate were mostly of the estates of rulers, warriors, scholars; a few only were theologians, tradesmen, husbandmen.

(Indignis quoque confertur.   Herostratus.)

2. Then it vexed me much that they admitted as many evil-doers (robbers, tyrants, adulterers, murderers, incendiaries, and so forth) as they did good men.   Then I understood that this could but encourage the perverse in their vices; and, indeed, it befell that one arrived claiming immortality who, asked what deed worthy of immortal memory he had done, replied that he had destroyed the most glorious thing in the world of which he knew; for he had purposely burnt down a temple on which seventeen kingdoms had during three centuries bestowed much labour and expense, and wrought its destruction in one day.   Then this man Censura was amazed at such infamous audacity, and, judging him unworthy, would not allow him to proceed.   But the Lady Fortuna came and ordered that he should be admitted.   Then, encouraged by this example, others enumerated all the awful deeds which they had committed.   One said that he had shed as much human blood as he could; another imagined a new form of blasphemy; another said that he had sentenced God to death; yet another said that he had torn down the sky from the firmament, and immersed it in an abyss; yet another had founded a new association of incendiaries and murderers through which the race of men was to be destroyed, and so forth. And all these were allowed to mount upward, which, I may say, greatly displeased me.

(*The Vanity of Fame.*)

3. Yet 1 followed them upward, and, behold, here an official of the Lady Fortuna, yclept Fama or Rumour, received them, and he consisted entirely of mouths. Indeed, as the one beneath [1] was full of eyes and ears, thus this one was all over full of mouths and tongues, from which no little sound and noise came forth; and this dear "Immortalitatis candidatus" derived at least that advantage therefrom, that through this noise his name became known far and wide. Now when I watched this somewhat carefully, I saw that the outcry that at first was raised over the name of each of these men first decreased and then ceased entirely, while cries referring to someone else were heard. "What immortality, then, is this?" quoth I; "each man abides here but for a span, then he again drifts away from theeyes, the mouths, the minds of men." The interpreter answered: "Thou dost belittle everything; but look, at least, at these men."

(*What Honour is there in figuring in History?*)

4. Then looking around, I behold painters who were sitting and gazing at these men and portraying them; then I asked: "Why do they this?" The interpreter answered: "That their names may not pass away and vanish as a voice; the memory of these men will endure." Then I gaze, and lo!

[1] *I.e.*, Censura.

each one of those who had been painted was then thrown into the abyss, just as the others; they left but the image, and that they placed on a pole, that it might be seen by all. " What immortality, then, is this ? " I said. " They leave here only the paper and the ink with which the man's name is daubed on the paper. The man himself perishes as miserably as other men. This is but deceit—dear God, deceit! What is that to me that one bedaubs me [1] on paper, if, meanwhile, I know not what befalls me. I give no import to this." Hearing this, the interpreter chides me as a madman, and asks me what purpose there is in the world for one whose thoughts were thus contrary to those of all others.

(*In History also there is much Falsehood.*)

5. Then I was silent, and lo! I discover a new falsehood. The image of one whom in life I had seen well shaped and handsome, was deformed; on the other hand, I saw that they had made the most beautiful image they could of one who was hideous; they made two, three, four images of one man, and each one was different; therefore both the carelessness and the faithlessness of these painters enraged me. I witness also the vanity of all this. For when I look at these pictures I see that many were so antiquated, dust-covered, mouldy, rotten, that one could recognise little or nothing at all; some could in the number hardly be distinguished from

[1] *I.e.*, my name.

the others [1]— at some hardly anyone looked.   This, then, is fame!

(*The Memorials of the Great also perish.*)

6. Meanwhile, Fortuna appeared, and ordered that some images, not only old and faded, but also new and fresh ones, should be thrown downward; then I understood that, just as this dear [2] immortality in itself is nothing, so also because of the mad fickleness of Fortuna (for she receives some in her castle, and then again expels them from it), no trust can be put in her; thus she and her gifts became more and more distasteful to me. For she dealt in the same fashion also with her sons when she walked about in her castle; to the voluptuous she sometimes gave delights, and then again took them from them; similarly she now granted the rich men riches; now deprived them of them; sometimes she took all from one and threw him downward out of her castle.

(*Then Death at last destroyed all.*)

7. Death also increased my terror when I saw her arrive at the castle, and remove now one man, now another, but in divers fashions. She shot at the rich with her usual arrows, or creeping towards them she strangled and suffocated them by means

---

[1] Every student of history will be struck by the accuracy of this remark.

[2] The word "dear" is often used ironically by Komensky.

of their chains.   She poured poison into the dainties
of the voluptuaries.   The famous she threw down
so that their heads broke, or struck them down by
means of swords, muskets, daggers; she led almost
all out of the world in some strange fashion.

CHAPTER XXVIII

THE PILGRIM BEGINS TO DESPAIR AND TO QUARREL
WITH HIS GUIDES

(Sapientiæ apex, desperatio de rebus mundi.)

Now, was I afeard, seeing that nowhere in the world,
not even in this castle, is there any enjoyment that
the mind can grasp safely, bravely, and entirely.
And this thought caused me to feel more and more
gloomy, and Falsehood, my guide, though he tried
all means, could not drive it from me. Indeed, I
exclaimed: "Oh! on my misery! Shall I, then,
never find any enjoyment in this wretched world?
Alas! everything is everywhere full of violence
and anxiety!" Then the interpreter says: "Whose
fault, then, is this, except thine own? thou loathsome, peevish one, who art disgusted with all that
ought to please thee. Behold the others, how each
one in his estate is gay and of good cheer, finding
sufficient sweetness in his pursuits." "Either,"
quoth I, "all these are mad, or they lie; for that
they enjoy true happiness is impossible." "Become
thou, then, mad too, that thou mayest relieve thy
anxiety." I answered: "I know not how to achieve
this; thou knowest that I have looked at many

things, but ever has the sight of the rapid changes in things, and their wretched purpose, driven me away."

(*In the World the Mind of Man findeth not that which it seeks.*)

2. Then the interpreter: " What but thy own imagination is the cause of this ? If thou didst not sift too curiously the ways of men, and argue all questions everywhere, thou wouldst, like the others, enjoy a quiet mind, pleasure, gladness, happiness." " Yes," I said, "if I clung to outward seemings, as thou hast; if I considered casual, tasteless laughter pleasure, thought the reading a few valueless books wisdom, and a small morsel of accidental felicity the summit of satisfaction. But why dost thou not take into account[1] the sweat, tears, groans, sickness, want, downfall, and other misfortunes that I see in all the estates, countless, measureless, endless ? Alas ! oh, alas ! Oh, over this miserable life ! You have led me everywhere, and what has it availed me ? It was promised me that I should be shown riches, learning, pleasure and security. But of all these things what have I ? Nothing ! What have I learnt ? Nothing ! Where am I ? That I myself know not. This only I know, that after so much struggling, so many labours, so much constant danger, so much fatigue and weariness of the mind, I find, at last, but wretchedness within me, and hatred of me in others ! "

[1] Literally, " where remain."

(Wherewith are Men misled and deceived?)

3. Then the interpreter: "It is well thus. Why wert thou not from the first guided by my counsel, which was to this purport: distrust nothing, believe everything, examine nothing, accept everything, revile nothing, find pleasure in everything? That would have been the path by which thou couldst have journeyed tranquilly, obtained the favour of others, and enjoyment for thyself." To this I answered: "No doubt this would have been a fine thing if, deceived by thee, I had maddened as the others; if I had rejoiced while erring to and fro; if, while groaning under the yoke, I had skipped; rejoiced, while sick and dying! I have seen and beheld and understood that I myself am nothing, understand nothing, possess nothing; neither do others; it is but a vain conceit. We grasp at the shadow, but truth ever escapes us. Oh, alas! and again alas!"

(He who looks through the World can but grieve.)

4. Then spake the interpreter: "What I have said before I will say yet again: 'Everything is thine own fault, for thou demandest somewhat great and unusual that no man obtains.'" I answered: "All the more do I grieve that not only I, but my whole race is wretched, and, being blind also, knoweth not its misery." Then the interpreter said: "I know not how and by what

means I can give satisfaction to thee and to thy addled brain. As neither the world nor men, neither work nor idleness, neither learning nor ignorance, nothing generally, pleases thee, I know not what to do with thee, nor what on all this world I can advise thee."

5. On this Impudence said: "Let us now lead him to the palace of our queen, which stands near here; there he will, perhaps, recover his reason."

CHAPTER XXIX

THE PILGRIM BEHOLDS THE PALACE OF WISDOM, THE QUEEN OF THE WORLD

THEN they take me and lead me on; and behold, the outer walls of this palace gleamed everywhere with divers beautiful paintings; and it had a gate at which guards stood; thus no one except those who had some power or office in the world could enter. To these only, as being servants of the queen and executors of her orders, liberty to go in and out was granted. Others, if they wished to behold the palace, had to gape at it from the outside only. (For it was said that it was not seemly that all should spy on the secrets by which the world is ruled.) And, indeed, of such who gaped at the castle from outside, more with their mouths than with their eyes, I saw a large number. None the less was I glad that they led me through the gates; for I had also always been desirous to know what secrets worldly Wisdom possessed.

2. But here also I was not without an accident; the guards, stopping me, begin to question me as to my purpose; indeed, they begin to drive and push me back, and to strike at me. But Impudence, who was well known here also, said I know not

what in my favour, and taking me by the hand, led me into the first court, all the same. Then looking at the building of the palace itself, I see white-gleaming walls which, they told me, were of alabaster; but looking at them carefully, and touching them with my hands, I find naught but paper, the crevices in which were stopped up by tow in every direction; herefrom I judged that these walls were but a hollow, artificial work. I wondered, and laughed at this deceit. We then came to the steps by which we were to go upward, and fearing destruction (and I think that my heart felt what would now befall me), I would not go on. Then the interpreter said: " Wherefore such fancies, my friend ? Then mayest thou also fear that the heavens will fall down on thee. Dost thou not see many who come and go upward and downward ? " Then, seeing here also examples in others, I went up this winding staircase, that was so high and round that giddiness might have befallen me.

CHAPTER XXX

HOW THE PILGRIM WAS IMPEACHED IN THE PALACE OF WISDOM

(The Pilgrim is placed before the Queen of Worldly Wisdom.)

THEN they lead me into a large hall, within which a wondrous lightness streamed towards me. It did not proceed from any of the many windows, but rather—as I was told—from the many precious stones with which the walls were encased; and the floor was bestrewn with precious carpets that also gleamed with gold, but in the place of a ceiling there appeared to be a cloud or mist. This I could not fully examine, for my eyes were incontinently fixed on the dear queen herself, who sat on the highest place under a baldachin; and around her stood on both sides her councillors and servants, a truly glorious company. But I was terrified by this splendour, and yet more so when the queen's ladies, one after the other, began to look at me. Then Impudence spake: "Fear naught; approach more closely, that her majesty the queen may see thee. Be then valiant, but forget not modesty nor courtesy." Then he led

Q

me into the middle of the hall and ordered me to
bow down low ; knowing not how to bear myself,
I did so.

(*The Pilgrim is impeached.*)

2. Then my interpreter, who, against my wishes,
had become my interpreter, began thus: "Most
serene queen of the world, most brilliant ray of
God's light, magnificent Wisdom! This young man
whom we bring before you has had the good
fortune to receive from Fate (the regent of your
Majesty) permission to view all the ranks and
conditions in this kingdom of the world, over which
the great God has placed you as His representative,
that you may by your prudence rule it wisely from
one boundary to the other. He has been led by
us, who, through your prudent decision, have been
appointed the guides of such men, through all the
estates of mankind. Yet—with humility and
sorrow we confess this to thee—in spite of all our
sincere and faithful endeavours, we have not
succeeded in persuading him to choose a certain
estate, establish himself tranquilly in it, and become
one of the faithful, obedient, constant inhabitants
of this our common country; rather is he ever
and on all occasions anxious, disgusted with all,
desirous of somewhat unusual. Therefore, as we
can neither satisfy his wild cravings nor even
understand them, we place him before your
illustrious serenitude, leaving it to your prudence
to decide what is to be done with him."

*(The Pilgrim is afeard. The Adversary; Power;
Endearment.* [1]*)*

3. Now everyone will judge what my state of
mind was when I heard this speech (which I had
not expected). For I now fully understood that I
had been brought here for judgment. Therefore
was I afeard; and yet more so when I saw lying
beneath the throne of the queen a terrible beast
(whether it was a dog or a lynx, or some dragon, I
do not well know); and when I saw that it looked
at me with sparkling eyes, I clearly saw that it
required little to incite it against me. There stood
there also two soldiers in mail, bodyguards of the
queen; they were indeed in female attire, but
terrible to behold, particularly the one who stood
at the left. For he wore an iron coat of mail,
prickly as a hedgehog (and even to touch it, I saw,
was dangerous); on his hands and feet he had
steely claws; in one hand he held a spear and a
sword, in the other arrows and fire-arms. The
second guard seemed to me laughable rather than
terrible; for instead of a coat of mail, he wore the
skin of a fox turned inward out; instead of a
halberd he carried the brush of a fox, and in the
left hand he held a nut-twig which he rattled.

(The Queen's Words to the Pilgrim.)

4. Now when my interpreter (or rather, if I may
say so, traitor) had finished his discourse, the queen

[1] For the explanation of these names, see later, p. 246.

(whose visage was covered by a most soft veil of lawn), spoke to me this weighty and lengthy speech: "Worthy young man, thy intention and desire to behold everything in the world displeaseth me not (indeed, I wish all my beloved ones to do this, and gladly through my trusty servants render them aid). But this I hear of thee with displeasure, that thou art somewhat fastidious; and though thou art in the world as a guest, who should learn what is new to him, yet thou givest thyself up to cavilling. Though I could therefore award thee punishment as an example to others, yet I wish that examples rather of my peaceableness and kindness than of my severity should be known to all; therefore I forbear with thee, and grant thee a residence near me in this my palace, that thou mayest better understand both thyself and the order of my rule. Value, then, this my favour, and learn that it is not granted to all to reach those secret spots, where the decrees and judgments of the world are delivered." When she had ended her speech she waved her hand, and I stepped aside, according to the instructions I had received, and I was anxious to see what now again would befall.

(*The Queen's Councillors.*)

5. Meanwhile, standing somewhat apart, I ask the interpreter how these councillors of the queen are named, what was the order among them, and what were the duties of each of them. Then he said to me: "Those privy councillors that stand

nearest to the queen are, at her right: Purity, Circumspection, Prudence, Caution, Affability, Moderation. On the left side stand: Truth, Zeal, Sincerity, Courage, Patience, and Constancy; and these are the councillors of the queen who ever surround her throne."

(*The Officials of the Queen.*)

6. "Now these who stand beneath the barriers are the queen's officials and vice-regents upon earth. The one who is clothed in grey garments is the ruler of the inferior regions, and she is called Industria or Endeavour; then that one garbed in purple, wearing a slighted necklace and a wreath (but her, I think, thou hast already seen) is the ruler of the Castle of Fame, and she is called the Lady Fortuna. These two and their aids are employed at their business, now here, now there; they have both to render services and to receive judgments and commands. Each of these has again her inferior officials under her; thus the Lady Industria has appointed Love to rule over the married people, Laboriousness over the trades and matters of commerce, Sagacity over the scholars, Piety over the clergy, Justice over the lawyers, and so forth."

(*The Rule of Women in the World.*)

7. Now hearing these fine names, and seeing that none the less all was awry in the world, I would

fain have spoken somewhat, but I dared not. I merely devised with myself: "This is indeed a wondrous government of the world. The king is a woman, the councillors are women, the officials are women; the whole rule is of women. How could anyone fear it?"

(*The Bodyguards.*)

8. Now I inquired also about these two body-guards, what and wherefore they were. He[1] said that her majesty the queen also had her enemies and caballers, against whom it behove her to guard herself. "This one in a fox's skin is called Endearment; the other, with iron and fire, is Power. When one cannot guard the queen, the other defends her; thus by turns they take the place one of the other. Then that dog who is near them does duty as watcher, who by barking makes known the approach of all who are suspect, and drives them away. He is known at Court as the Messenger, but those whom his duties please not much call him the Adversary. But cease now to gape; listen and attend to what will befall here." "It is well," said I, "with pleasure."

[1] *I.e.*, the interpreter.

CHAPTER XXXI

SOLOMON, WITH A LARGE MULTITUDE, COMES TO THE PALACE OF WISDOM

*(Solomon comes forward, wishing to obtain Wisdom
as his Spouse.)*

Now when I prepare to listen to what was to befall
here, a great noise and tumult arises, and as all
looked round, I also did thus. And I see, entering
the palace, one clothed in bright splendour, bearing
a crown and a golden sceptre, and a huge company
followed him. All were afeard, and the eyes of all
—mine also—were turned to him. Then approaching nearer, he declared that he had thus been
honoured by the highest God of gods, that he
could behold the world more freely than all who
had come before him or would come after him, and
more than this, that he would take Wisdom, the
ruler of the world, for wife; therefore had he
sought her.

(And he called himself Solomon, the King of the
Israelite Nation, the most glorious one under
Heaven. What was answered to him, and
what he then again said.—Eccl. ii. 7.)

2. Then through Prudence, the chancellor of the
queen, he received this reply, that Wisdom was the
spouse of Christ Himself, and could not wed any
other; but that if he wished to find favour with her,
this would not be refused to him. Then Solomon
said : "Now will I strive to see what difference
there is between wisdom and folly; for nothing
pleaseth me that happens under the sun."

(*The Pilgrim rejoices.*)

3. Oh, how greatly I rejoiced, hearing that
now at last—God be thanked!—I should obtain
a guide and councillor different from those I
had had before, one with whom I could dwell
safely, with whose help I could examine everything, and whom, lastly, I could follow where he
went. And I began to praise God within my
mind.

(*Solomon's Company.*)

4. Now, Solomon had with him a vast company
of servitors and friends, who came with him to
behold Wisdom, this queen of the world. Among

those around him there were honourable men of worthy habit, of whom I was told, on inquiring, that they were called patriarchs, prophets, apostles, confessors, and so forth. Further back amidst the crowd they showed me some of the philosophers— Socrates, Plato, Epictetus, Seneca, and others. They all sat down at both sides of the hall, and I did so also, with great expectation of what would befall.

CHAPTER XXXII

THE PILGRIM BEHOLDS THE SECRET JUDGMENTS AND THE GOVERNMENT OF THE WORLD

Now I soon understood that those matters common to all estates only were administered here; the more private ones were settled, each in its own place, in town-halls, law-courts, consistories, and so forth. But what now befell in my presence I will make known as briefly as possible.

(*Complaints of the Disorders of the World.*)

2. First, the two officials or vice-regents of the world, Industria and Fortuna, came forward and spake of the disorders that come to pass in all the estates; these, they said, were caused by the general faithlessness, craftiness, plots and frauds; and they begged that in some manner this be righted. And I rejoiced, seeing that they also understood what I understood, namely, that there is no order in this world. Remarking this, the interpreter said: "Thou hadst then believed that thou alone hast eyes, and that except thee no man seeth aught. Well, see now how carefully those to whom this duty is entrusted attend to those

matters!" "Gladly do I hear this," I said. "May God but grant that the right path be found!"

(They seek for the Causes of the Disorders of the World.)

3. Then I saw that the councillors assembled, and after they had held council together they decided that through the chancellor Prudence the question be put whence these disorders arose. And after much investigation it was stated that some rioters and mutineers had stolen in who secretly and openly spread disorder. The greatest blame was awarded (for they were all mentioned by name) to Drunkenness, Greed, Usury, Lust, Pride, Cruelty, Laziness, Idleness, and some others.

(A Decree is issued against the Causers of these Disorders.)

4. They then again took council about these, and at last they came to a decision that was read out, and that declared that it should, through open charters, that were to be hung up in certain places and sent to all parts of the land, be made known that her majesty, Queen Wisdom, had remarked that through the many strangers who had slyly stolen into the land, many disorders also had found entrance into it. Therefore she declared that those who were found to be the ringleaders should, for all times, be expelled from her kingdom, particularly Drunkenness, Greed, Usury,

Lust, and others; from this very hour they should no longer allow themselves to be seen, under penalty of immediate death. When this decree was issued by means of the charters that had been prepared, wondrous jubilation began among the joyful people; each one—and I also—now looked forward to the golden age.

(*New Complaints and New Decrees.*)

5. But when, after a while, nothing became better in the world, many hurriedly came forward, complaining that the decree had not been carried out. After the council had again met, the queen appointed as her special commissioners Heednot and Overlook, and in view of the great importance of the matter, Moderation, one of the queen's councillors was to join them; they were instructed to carefully investigate whether some of these evil-reputed exiles had remained in the land contrarily to the decree of banishment, or had audaciously returned. Then the commissioners went their way, and returning some time afterwards, they reported that they had indeed found some who appeared suspect; but these did not count themselves among the men who had been banished, and indeed bore different names. One who appeared similar to Drunkenness was named Tipsiness or Merriment; one who resembled Greed was called Economy; a third, similar to Usury, bore the name of Interest; a fourth, who resembled Lust, was called Love; a fifth, similar to Pride, was named Dignity; a

sixth resembled Cruelty, but his name was Severity; a seventh, similar to Laziness, was named Good-nature, and so forth.

(The Charters are expounded.)

6. After this matter had been considered by the council, it was now decreed that Merriment was not to be called Drunkenness, nor Economy Greed, and so forth. Therefore the persons named were to be left free, as the charter concerned them not. As soon as this decision was made known, these incontinently walked abroad freely, and a crowd of common folk who followed them became acquainted with them, and associated with them. Looking now at Solomon and his companions, I see that they shake their heads; but as these men were silent, I also was silent; but I heard one of them whisper to another: " The names (they say) are banished, but the traitors and destroyers, after changing their names, have free access. This will not end well!"

(The Estates of the World demand greater Liberties.)

7. And now envoys of all the estates of the world came forth and demanded audience; when admitted they presented, with strange gestures, this humble entreatment: " Would Her Majesty, the most Ilustrious Queen, deign graciously to remember how faithfully and obediently all the loyal estates of the realm had clung to the sceptre of her rule, consenting wholly to her rights, decrees, and command over

all; now also they were of this and no other intent; only they humbly begged that, as a reward for past, and as an encouragement for future and stable fidelity, Her Royal Majesty would grant them some increase of their privileges and liberties, according to the fashion that pleased H. R. M.[1] They promised that they would, by constant obedience, prove their gratitude for this gift." Then they finished speaking, bowed to the earth, and withdrew. Then rubbing my eyes, I said unto myself: " What will this be ? Has the world, then, not enough of liberty that it demands more ? A bridle you require, a bridle and a whip, and somewhat of hellebore." But I devised thus with myself only, for I had decided to say naught; in the presence of these sages and grey-haired men, this was more beseeming for me.

(*The Distribution of New Privileges.*)

8. And they again meet in council, and after much deliberation the queen gave it to be known that she had ever striven to educate and to adorn her kingdom, and that of her own free will she was inclined to this; having then heard the prayers of her trusty and well-beloved subjects, she did not wish to leave them unfulfilled. Therefore had she decided to improve their titles, that they might be more greatly honoured. Thus would they more clearly and by greater honour be distin-

[1] I follow Komensky's example in using here the initials only.

guished the one from the other.   Therefore did she decree and ordain that henceforth the tradesmen should be called "renowned," the students "illustrious" and "most learned," the masters of arts and doctors "most renowned," the priests "reverend," "praiseworthy," or "worthy of all honour"; the bishops "most saintly," the richer among the citizens "gentle," the country gentlemen "gentle and valiant knights," the lords "two-fold lords,"[1] the counts "high-born lords and lords,"[1] the princes "most potent," the kings "most splendid and invincible."   "That this be more firmly established, I decree that none shall be obliged even to receive a letter if any part of his title be omitted or it be worded wrongly."   Then the envoys went forth, after giving the queen thanks.   And I thought within myself : "Noble booty have you obtained ; lines on a morsel of paper."

(*The Humble Supplications of the Poor.*)

9. Now, the poor of all ranks came forth with a supplication, in which they complained of the great inequality in the world, and that others had abundance while they suffered want.   They begged that this might in some fashion be righted.   After the matter had been weighed, it was decreed that the poor should be told in answer that H.R M.

[1] The custom of twice repeating a title as a proof of respect — still occasionally met with in Bohemia — was general in Komensky's time ; an example will be found in his dedication of this book to Charles, Lord of Zerotin.

wished indeed that all should have as much comfort as they could themselves desire, but that the glory of the kingdom demanded that the light of some should shine above that of others. Therefore, in accordance with the order established in the world, it could not be otherwise than that as Fortuna had her castle, so also should Industria have her workshops full of people. But this was granted them, that each one who was not idle might raise himself from poverty by whatever means he could or knew.

(The Supplications of the Industrious Ones.)

10. Now, when the answer given to these supplicants became known, others after a while appeared bearing a petition of the industrious. They begged that in future those who idled not should be assured, whatever their estate and their enterprises might be, that they would obtain that for which they strove and worked, and that blind fortune should not decide. Concerning this petition, a lengthy council was held; thence I judged that the matter was by no means an easy one. At last it was declared that, though the power and might that had once been entrusted to Fortuna and her faithful servant Chance (for it could not be otherwise) could not be taken out of their hands, yet their petition would be remembered, and an order given that, as far as possible, the industrious rather than the thriftless should be

considered; they could therefore act in accordance with this.   And they also went forth.

(The Supplications of the Learned and Famous.)

11. Immediately afterwards followed the envoys of some illustrious men.   They were Theophrastus and Aristotle, and they asked for two things : firstly, that they should not be subject to the accidents of life as other men are; secondly, as they were, through God's kindness, distinguished by great wit, learning, riches, and so forth, above all others in the world (and as it would be a general loss should such men perish), they begged for this privilege above the common multitude : that they should never die.   After their first request had been considered, they were told that they demanded just things; they would therefore be allowed to protect themselves against accidents as well as they could; the learned by means of their learning, the prudent by their prudence, the powerful by their power, the rich by their riches.   With regard to their second demand, Queen Wisdom gave the order that all the most renowned alchemists should be assembled, and should with all diligence study the means by which immortality could be obtained. Then those who received this order withdrew.   But when after a time none of them returned, and the envoys pressed for an answer, they received, *pro interim*, a message to the purpose that H.R.M. did not desire that such precious men should perish together with the others; but that she knew not

R

for the moment how to accomplish this. This privilege should, however, be given to them, that while the others were buried immediately after death, these should be kept among the living as long as possible ; while the others would after death be merely under a green sod, these would repose under stones. This and what else they could imagine to distinguish themselves from the common rabble was to be granted them, and a charter given them to that import.

(*Supplications of the Rulers.*)

12. When these had departed, some came forward as representatives of the rulers ; they dilated on the hardships of that estate, and asked for relief. Then permission was granted them to seek rest, and rule by means of their vice-regents and officials ; they acquiesced in this, and departed, after giving thanks.

(*Supplications of the Subjects.*[1])

13. Not long afterwards envoys of the subjects, tradesmen, and peasants came forward, and complained that those who were over them wished nothing but to drink their sweat ; for they ordered them to be so driven and harassed that bloody sweat ran down them. And those whom the lords

---

[1] *I.e.*, serfs.

employed for such purposes [1] were all the more
cruel to them, that they also might obtain a small
dish at their expense.   And as a proof of this they
incontinently showed countless weals, stripes, scars,
and wounds ; and they asked for mercy.   And it
appeared evident that this was an injustice, and
therefore should be stopped ; but as the rulers had
been permitted to govern by means of these
servants, it appeared that they were the guilty
ones ; they were therefore summoned to appear.
Summonses were therefore sent out to all the royal,
princely, and lordly councillors, regents, officials,
stewards, collectors, writers, judges, and so forth,
informing them that they must appear without fail.
They obeyed the order, but against one accusation they brought forward ten.   They complained of the laziness of the peasants, their
disobedience, insubordination, conceit, their mis-
chievous ways as soon as their bit was even
slightly loosened, and other things.   After these
men had been heard, the whole matter was again
considered by the council.   Then the subjects were
told that, as they either did not love and value the
favour of their superiors, or were unable to obtain
it, they must become used to their ferocity ; for
thus must it be in the world, that some rule and
others serve.   Yet it was granted them, that if by
willingness, compliance, and true attachment to

---

[1] Komensky here refers to the officials whom the Bohemian
lords appointed to rule their peasants ; these officials had an
evil reputation of cruelty and dishonesty.

their superiors and rulers they could gain their favour, they should be allowed to enjoy it.

(The Grievances of the Jurists and Advocates.— Ratio Status is given them as a Precept.)

14. After these had been dismissed, there remained the jurists (councillors of the kings and lords, doctors of laws, advocates, judges, and so forth) who complained of the incompleteness of written laws,[1] in consequence of which not all the disputes that arose among men could be decided (though they already noted more than a hundred thousand cases). Thus it happened that they were either unable to maintain perfect order among men, or—if they added somewhat out of their own minds for the purpose of expounding the law and ending strife—the unwise considered this to be a misrepresentation of the law, and a perversion of their case ; thence they incurred dislike, and litigation increased among them. They therefore demanded either advice as to their behaviour, or protection against the forward judgments of men. Then, after they had been told to withdraw, the matter was discussed ; but it would be long to tell what the pleading of each of the queen's councillors was. Therefore will I only tell of the decision that was made known to the jurists after they had again been called forward—to wit, that H.R.M.

---

[1] The jurists demanded the complete codification of the laws.

knew no way by means of which new laws applying
to all possible cases could be written down, therefore should the former laws and customs remain in
force.   But H.R.M. deigned to give them this
rule and key, that when expounding the laws and
passing judgment in accordance with them, they
should seek either their own advantage or that of
the community.   This rule was to be called Ratio
Status; by means of it they would be able to
guard themselves as with a shield against the
thrusts of vulgar calumny.   The fashion of rule
(which not all could understand) required that
some things should remain as they were.   The
jurists, having received this their new rule,
promised to conform to it and withdrew.

*(Complaints of the Women against the Men, and the
Men against the Women.)*

15. But a short time passed, and then the women
came, complaining that they had to live under the
rule of men, as if they were slaves.   Immediately
afterwards men also were found who lamented over
the disobedience of women.   Then the queen and
her advisers met in council more than once.   Then
through the lady chancellor this answer was issued:
" As Nature had given man superiority, this should
remain as it was, but under these important restric-
tions : firstly, as women form half the human race,
men shall do naught without hearing their counsel ;
secondly, as Nature often pours out her gifts more
bounteously on women than on men, every woman

whose wit and strength enabled her to lord it over her lord should be called 'amazon,'[1] and the man should not be allowed to take the supremacy from her." This was the first answer, but neither men nor women were content with it. The women, indeed, wished that the men should either share the rule with them, or that they should take it by turns; thus would the command change, and be held, now by the men, now by the women. Some even were found who wished nothing less than that women alone should rule, alleging their greater agility both of mind and of body; therefore, as men had for so many thousand years had supremacy, it was time that they should cede it to the women. And, indeed, a few years since, in the English Kingdom, a noble example of this was seen.[2] When Queen Elizabeth ruled, she decreed that men should give their right hand to women[3] to honour them, and this worthy custom still endured. As therefore H.M. Wisdom, the queen of the world, and all her lady-councillors, had by God been created in this their sex, and yet placed over men as their rulers,

[1] This passage is very difficult to translate; the literal meaning of the Bohemian "muzatka" would be "manness" (the German "männin").

[2] Comp. "Il governo delle donne ha avuta la prevalenza nel nostro secolo; nuove amazoni sono comparse tra la Nubia e la Monopotama e in Europa noi abbiamo veduto regnare Roxolane in Turchia, Buona in Polonia, Maria in Ungheria, Elisabetta in Inghilterra, Catterina in Francia, Bianca in Toscana, Margherita nel Belgio, Maria in Scozia, Isabella che favorì la scoperta del nuovo mondo in Spagna." —Campanella, "Civitas Solis," Italian translation, Lugano, 1850.

When leading them into a room.

it appeared seemly. (" Regis ad exemplum totus componi orbus.") [1] The same rule as in the world should prevail in houses and communities also. By this speech they thought that they would easily guide the mind of Queen Wisdom to their own view.   Then the men, not to lose their case by their silence, opposed this; they said that though God had entrusted the government of the world to Queen Wisdom, yet He mainly held it Himself in His own hands, therefore would they do so also, and so forth.

(An Agreement between Men and Women.)

16. Then they again met in council several times, and thus I understood that they had never had so grave a matter brought before them. Though we were all waiting for the final decision, we received it not; but Prudence and Affability were instructed to deliberate secretly with both parties. These, mediating in the matter, found a compromise, namely, that for the purpose of peace and harmony in their homes, men should at least tacitly grant superiority to the women, and avail themselves of their advice ; the women, contenting themselves with this, should outwardly appear obedient. Thus things would seemingly remain as before, yet the domestic rule of women would be strengthened ; for otherwise the great secret that

[1] The Latin words are printed thus in Mr. Bily's last edition (founded on the Amsterdam MS.), and also in Mr. Korinek's recent edition of the " Labyrinth."

men rule the community, and women again rule men, might become apparent. The queen begged both parties to prevent this; this was agreed to on both sides. Then, seeing this, one of Solomon's companions said (Syr. xxvi. 29[1]): "A woman who honours her husband is considered wise!" and a second added (Ephes. v. 23): "The husband is the head of the wife, even as Christ is the head of the Church." But the friendly agreement was confirmed, and both men and women withdrew.

[1] From the Apocrypha.

CHAPTER XXXIII

SOLOMON DISCLOSES THE VANITIES AND DECEITS OF THE WORLD

(The Mask of Worldly Wisdom is Uncovered.—
Eccl. i. 2, 15.)

THEN Solomon, who had hitherto sat looking on quietly, could no longer contain himself. With a loud voice, he began to cry: "Vanity of vanities; all is vanity! Cannot that which is crooked be made straight; and that which is wanting be numbered?" Then he rose, and with him his whole following, with great tumult; and he went straight to the throne of the queen. And neither this fierce beast, the Messenger, nor the guards on both sides could prevent this; for his voice and his splendour intimidated them all, and, indeed, the queen, also, and her councillors. Then he stretched out his hand and took from her face the veil which had before appeared costly and glittering, but now appeared as nothing but a spider's web. And behold! her face was pale, but swollen; there was indeed some red on her cheeks, but it was paint; and this appeared clearly, for in some places it had peeled off; the hands also appeared

scabby, the whole body displeasing, and her breath
stank. Then I, and all the others present, were so
afeard that we were almost benumbed.

(*Her Councillors also are unmasked.*—Eccl. i. 14.)

2. Then Solomon turned to the councillors of the
pretended queen, took their masks from them, and
said : " I see that in the place of justice, injustice
rules, and abomination in that of sanctity. Your
carefulness is distrust, your foresight cunning, your
affability flattery, your truth self-deceit ; your zeal
is fury, your valour foolhardiness, your love lust,
your work slavery, your sagacity mere conjecture,
your religion hypocrisy, and so forth. Is it, then,
your task to rule the world instead of the Almighty
God ? God will bring to judgment all deeds and
all secret things, be they good or bad. But I will
go forth and announce this to the whole world, that
it may no longer permit itself to be misguided and
misled."

(*Solomon proclaims the Vanity of the World to the
whole World.*)

3. Then turning round, he went forth wrath-
fully, and his companions with him ; then when
he began to cry out, " Vanity of vanities, and all
is vanity ! " then from all directions men of all
countries and nations, kings and queens from
distant lands, collected around him. And his
eloquence rained down on them and instructed

them, for his words were as thorns and nails
that are driven home.

(They hold Counsel as to how they could outwit him.)

4. But I followed them not, but remained in the
palace, standing with my guides, who were horror-
stricken, and beheld everything that further befell
there. The queen, namely, who had recovered from
her faint, began to take counsel with her councillors
as to what should be done. Zeal, Sincerity, and
Courage advised that all the forces should be collected and sent in pursuit of Solomon, that he
might be captured. Prudence, on the contrary,
declared that no good would be done by means
of violence; for not only was Solomon himself
also powerful, but he had almost the whole world
as his following. Thus did the messengers, who,
one after the other, brought news of what had
happened, report; rather should Affability and
Flattery be sent after him, and they should take
Pleasure with them from Fortuna's castle; wherever he was, they should trickishly enwind themselves round him, showing and praising the beauty
and loveliness of the kingdom of the world. "Thus,
perhaps," Prudence said, "he could be caught;
another way she knew not." And it was ordered
that these three should set out at once.

CHAPTER XXXIV

SOLOMON IS DECEIVED AND MISLED

(Solomon rains forth Wisdom.)

Now, seeing this, I tell my guides that I also would gladly behold what was to befall. Impudence immediately consented, and went forth; the interpreter did likewise. Then, when we had set out, we find Solomon with his companions in the street of the scholars; and to the wonder of all, he conversed of the nature of trees, from the cedar tree that is in Lebanon even unto the hyssop that springeth out of the wall. He spake also of beasts, and of fowl, and of creeping things, and of fishes; of the nature of the earth, the power of the elements, the constellations, the thoughts of men, and so forth. And men came from all nations to listen to his wisdom. Being thus extolled beyond all measure himself, he began to delight in himself; this all the more when Affability and Flattery, cautiously approaching him, began yet further to increase his praise before the eyes of men.

(Solomon devises Learned Crafts.)

2. Then he rose up and went forth to behold other parts of the world, and entering the street of the tradesmen, he began to wonder at their divers arts, and to find pleasure in them; then with his deep wit he devised for them strange things, such as the artful fashioning of gardens, orchards, fishponds, the building of houses and towns, and the furthering of all that delights mankind.

(He is entangled into the State of Matrimony.)

3. Now, when Solomon entered the street of the married people, Pleasure cunningly led to him all the most beautiful maidens, adorned in the most beauteous manner with divers sweet-sounding music. She told some of the most lovely to welcome the king solemnly, and they greeted him as the light of the human race, the crown of the Israelite nation, the jewel of the world; "as the estate of the scholars, as well as that of the tradesmen, had," they said, "gained not little from the presence of his light and illumination, thus did the estate of matrimony also strive to obtain through his presence an increase of its glory." After thanking courteously, Solomon said that he intended to honour that estate by joining it; then choosing from among the maidens her who seemed to him most beautiful, he consented to be weighed together with her,[1] and linked to her

[1] *See* chapter viii.

(they called her the daughter of Pharaoh). Abiding now with her, he was struck by her beauty, and sought rather her glance and pleasure than wisdom ; then (a thing I should never have imagined) he allowed his glances to fall on the crowd of joyous maidens—and cunning Pleasure brought more and yet more of them before his eyes ; struck by the beauty now of this, now of that one, he called to him all that came in his way, without their even being weighed together. Thus, in a short time he beheld seven hundred of them[1] around him, and three hundred also that were not wedded ; for he held it as glory to surpass, in such matters also, all who were before him and would be after him. And now nothing was to be seen but amorous trifling, and even his own followers grieved and groaned over this.

(He now visits the Estate of Priesthood, and there sinks entirely.)

4. Now, when he had passed through this street he proceeded farther, and entered the street of the priests, and whither the wretched companions who were fettered to him dragged him, thither he allowed himself to be drawn among beasts and reptiles, dragons and poisonous vermin ;[2] and he began to find doleful delight among them.

---

[1] *I.e.*, wives.
[2] Of course, an allusion to Solomon's idolatry.

CHAPTER XXXV

SOLOMON'S COMPANY IS DISPERSED AND CAPTURED, AND PERISHES BY TERRIBLE FASHIONS OF DEATH

(Solomon's Companions express Displeasure.)

SEEING Solomon thus deceived, those who were the foremost among his following—Moses, Elias, Isaias, Jeremias—began to speak with great zeal; they protested before heaven and earth that they would take no part in such abominations, and they admonished the whole following to refrain from such vanity and folly. But as no few, none the less, followed Solomon's example, their ire became yet more inflamed, and they thundered yet more furiously, particularly Isaias, Jeremias, Baruch, Stephen, Paul, and others. Moses demanded that those with him should gird on their swords; Elias that fire should come downward from heaven; Ezechias that all those idols should be destroyed.

(They heed not Wheedling Speech.)

2. Seeing this, those who had been sent forth to mislead Solomon—Affability, Flattery, and Pleasure, taking with them some of the philoso-

phers, Mammon, and others—advised the zealots to moderate themselves and behave in a more temperate fashion. When the wisest of men, Solomon, had submitted his mind and become accustomed to the ways of the world, why should they walk apart from the others, and continue to cavil? But this advice was not heard; the more they saw that Solomon's example misled and deceived many, the more they angered, ran to and fro, screamed and raged; and this matter caused great riot.

(*Public Forces are sent against them.*)

3. For the queen, who had been advised of all this by her attendants, issued charters by which she summoned all men to her aid. Power, the leader of her bodyguard, was appointed general, and ordered to arrest the rioters and punish them as a warning to all. Then the alarm was sounded, and many assembled, prepared for the war, not only men of the estate of the mercenaries, but also magistrates, officials, judges, tradesmen, philosophers, physicians, lawyers, and even priests; women even went forth in divers dresses and with divers arms (for it was said that against such public enemies of the world all must give their aid, be they young or old). Seeing this vast army rolling along, I ask my guides: "What will now befall?" Then the interpreter: "Now wilt thou learn what is the fate of those who, by their cavilling, cause riots and conspiracies among men."

*(Battle, Captivity, Murder, Burning, and other
Torture.)*

4. Then these men, attacking now one, then a second, a third, a tenth, strike, cut, and knock them down, trample them underfoot, capture them, bind them, lead them to prison, according to the greatness of their fury against each one of them. It is wondrous that my heart broke not from pity; but though terrified by such cruelty and quivering, I yet dared not budge. Then I see that some of those who had been imprisoned and struck down wrung their hands, craving pardon for their deeds; while others maintained their opinions, however cruelly they were treated. Then, incontinent, some were before my eyes cast into the fire; others thrown into the water, hanged, decapitated, crucified, tortured with pincers, sawed, pierced, chopped, roasted on gridirons—I cannot, indeed, number all the cruel forms of death that these men suffered; but the worldly ones rejoiced and exulted over this.

CHAPTER XXXVI

THE PILGRIM DESIRES TO FLEE FROM THE WORLD

(The Pilgrim flees the World.)

THEN, unable to behold such sights or to bear the sorrows of my heart any longer, I fled, wishing to seek refuge in some desert, or rather, were it but possible, to escape from the world. But my guides pursued me, overtook me, and asked me whither I intended to go. Wishing to reprove them by silence, I answered naught. But when they, not wishing to leave me, continued mischievously to pursue me, I said: "I see now that matters will not become better in the world. All my hopes are ended. Woe on me!" Then they: "Wilt thou not think better of it, after having seen what is the fate of those who cavil?" Then I answered: "Thousandfold do I prefer to die, rather than to be where such things befall, and to behold vice, lies, corruption, cruelty. Therefore is death to me more desirable than life. I shall set out and see what is the fate of the dead whom I see carried forth."

(*Falsehood disappears.*)

2. Impudence immediately granted my request,
saying that it was well that I should see and
understand such things also. The other dissuaded
me, and endeavoured to stop me ; but heeding him
not, I tore myself away and proceeded on my way.
Then he remained there and forsook me.

(*The Pilgrim beholds the Dying and Dead. The
Bottomless Abyss beyond the World.*)

3. Looking now about me, I behold the ways of
the dying, of whom there were many ; and I see a
mournful thing—to wit, that all gave up the ghost
with horror, lamentation, fear and trembling, knowing not what would befall them and whither they
would go. Although I was afeard, yet wishing
ever to acquire more knowledge, I walked through
the rows of the dead to the limits of the world and
of light. Here, where others, shutting their eyes,
blindly cast forth their dead, I threw off the
glasses of Falsehood, rubbed my eyes, and leaned
forward as far as I dared. And I behold awful
darkness and gloom, of which the mind of man
can find neither the end nor the ground ; and
there was here naught but worms, frogs, serpents,
scorpions, rottenness, stench, the smell of brim-
stone and pitch that overwhelmed body and soul,
generally unspeakable horror.

(The Pilgrim falls to the Ground terrified.)

4. Then my bowels quaked, my whole body trembled, and, terrified, I fell swooning to the ground, and cried mournfully: "Oh, most miserable, wretched, unhappy mankind! this, then, is your last glory! this the conclusion of your many splendid deeds! this the term of your learning and much wisdom over which you glory so greatly! this the rest and repose that you crave after countless labours and struggles! this the immortality for which you ever hope! Oh, that I had never been born, never passed through the gate of life! For after the many vanities of the world; nothing but darkness and horror are my part! O God, God, God! God, if Thou art a God, have mercy on wretched me!"

THE PARADISE OF THE HEART[1]

CHAPTER XXXVII

THE PILGRIM FINDS HIS WAY HOME

(The First Conversion is the Work of God.)

Now, when I cease speaking, and am still shaking with fear, I hear above me a mysterious voice that said "Return!" And I lift my head to see who was calling; but I see nothing, not even my guide Searchall; for he, too, had now forsaken me.

2. And lo! now a voice again resounded "Return!" Then knowing not how to turn back, nor whither to go out of this darkness, I began to sorrow, when lo! the voice again called: "Return whence thou camest to the house of the heart, and then close the doors behind thee."

[1] As I have already mentioned, Komensky has not indicated the division of his book into two parts by any external signs; the numbering of the chapters and pages continues uninterrupted throughout the whole work.

(The Second Conversion requires our own Endeavours also.)

3. This counsel I obeyed as well as I could, and it was well with me that I thus obeyed God, who had counselled me; but this was yet a gift from Him. Then collecting my thoughts as best I could, I closed my eyes, ears, mouth, nostrils, and abandoned all contact with external things. Then I entered into the innermost of my heart, and behold! everything therein was darkness. But when, with blinking eyes, I gaze a little around me, I behold a weak light that penetrated through the crevices; and I see above me, in the vaulting of this my little chamber, what appeared to me a large, round, glassy window; but it had been so much soiled and bedaubed that scarce any light came through it.

(Description of Corrupt Nature.)

4. Then, looking around me by means of this dim, scant light, I see on the walls certain small pictures of, as it seemed, sometime pretty work; but the colours had faded, and some portions of the pictures had been hewn off, or broken off. Approaching them more closely, I see on them inscriptions such as Prudence, Meekness, Justice, Chastity, Temperance, and so forth. Then in the middle of the chamber I see divers broken and damaged ladders, and pincers and ropes, that had been damaged and scattered about; item, large

wings with plucked plumes ; lastly, clock-works
with broken or bent cylinders, dents, and little
columns ; and all this was scattered about at
random, here and there.

*(Corrupt Nature cannot be mended by Worldly
Wisdom.)*

5. And I wondered what was the purpose of
these implements, how and by whom they had
been injured, and how they could be repaired.
Now thinking of this and considering it, I could
devise naught; but hope arose in me that He who
by His call had led me to this chamber, whoever
He might be, would again address me, and further
instruct me. For that of which I had here seen
but the beginning pleased me well, both because
my little chamber had not the evil smell of the
other places, through which I had passed in the
world, and also because I found not here rustle and
rush, noise and crash, unrest and reeling to and fro,
tussling and violence (things of which the world is
full). Here everything was quiet.

CHAPTER XXXVIII

THE PILGRIM RECEIVES CHRIST AS HIS GUEST

(Our Illumination cometh from on High.)

I now devise of this with myself, and wait what will further befall. And behold, a clear light appeared on high, and raising my eyes towards it, I see the window above me full of brightness, and from out of that brightness there appeared One, in aspect, indeed, similar to a man, but in His splendour truly God. His countenance shone exceedingly, yet could human eyes gaze at it, for it caused not terror; rather had it a loveliness such as I had never seen in the world. He then—kindness itself, friendliness itself—addressed me in these most sweet words :

(Wherein the Source of all Light and all Joy lieth.)

2. " Welcome, welcome, my son and dear brother." And having said these words, He embraced me, and kissed me kindly. There came forth from Him a most delightful odour, and I was seized by such unspeakable delight that tears flowed from my eyes, and I knew not how to

respond to so unexpected a greeting. Only sighing deeply, I gazed at Him with meek eyes. Then He, seeing me overwhelmed with joy, spoke thus further to me: " Where, then, has thou been, my son ? why hast thou tarried so long ? by what path hast thou come ? what hast thou sought in the world ? Joy ! where could thou seek it but in God ; and where couldst thou seek God, but in His own temple ; and what is the temple of the living God, but the living temple that He Himself has fashioned—thine own heart ? I saw, my son, that thou wentest astray, but I would see it no longer. I have brought thee to thy own self. I have led thee into thyself. For here have I chosen my palace and my dwelling. If thou wishest here to dwell with me, thou wilt find here, what thou hast vainly sought on earth, rest, comfort, glory, and abundance of all things. This I promise thee, my son, that thou wilt not be deceived here as thou wert there in the world."

(*The Pilgrim gives himself over entirely to Jesus.*)

3. Hearing such speech, and understanding that He who spake was my Redeemer, Jesus Christ, of whom I had indeed heard somewhat in the world, but superficially only, I folded my hands, and then stretched them out, not, as in the world, with fear and doubt, but with full happiness and complete faith ; then I said : " I am here, my Lord Jesus ; take me to Thee. Thine I wish to be, and to remain for ever. Speak to Thy servant, and

permit me to hear Thee; tell me what Thou desirest, and grant that I find pleasure in it; lay on me what burden Thou thinkest fit, and grant that I may bear it; employ me for whatever purpose Thou desirest, and grant me that I may not be found wanting; order me to act according to Thy will, and grant me grace to do so. Let me be nothing, that Thou mayest be everything."

CHAPTER XXXIX

THEIR BETROTHAL

(God's Wisdom directs even our Errors.)

"I ACCEPT this from thee, my son," quoth He.
"Hold to this, become, call thyself, and remain
mine own. Mine, indeed, thou wert and art from
all eternity, but thou knewest it not. I have long
prepared for thee that happiness to which I will
now lead thee; but thou didst not understand this.
I have led thee to thyself through strange paths
and by roundabout ways; this thou knewest not,
nor what I, the ruler of all my chosen ones,
intended; neither didst thou perceive by what
means I worked on thee. But I was everywhere
with thee, and therefore somewhat guided thee
through these crooked paths, that I might at last
bring thee yet closer to me. Naught could the
world, naught thy guides, naught Solomon teach
thee. They could by no means enrich thee, content
thee, satisfy the desires of thy heart, for they had
not that which thou didst seek. But I will teach
thee everything, enrich thee, content thee."

(*All Worldly Striving should be transferred to God.*)

2. " This only I demand of thee, that whatever
thou hast seen in the world, and whatever struggles
thou hast witnessed among men, thou shouldst
transfer it to me, and lay the burden of it on me.
This, as long as thou livest, shall be thy work and
thy task ; of that which men seek there in the
world, but find not—to wit, peace and joy—I will
give thee abundance."

(*The Pilgrim joins Christ only, his Eternal Spouse.*)

3. "Thou hast seen in the estate of the married
people how those who find pleasure in one another
leave everything, that they may belong to each
other. Do thus thou also, leave everything, even
thyself ; give thyself up fully to me, and thou
wilt be mine, and it will be well. As long as
thou dost not this, thou wilt, I assure thee,
obtain no solace for thy soul. For in the world
everything changeth ; everything beside me for
which thy mind and thy desire will strive, will,
in one way or another, cause thee toil and dis-
content ; at last it will forsake thee, and the
joy that thou hadst found in it will turn to woe.
Therefore I faithfully counsel thee, my son, forsake everything and cling to me ; be mine, and I
thine. Let us shut ourselves up together here in
this shrine, and thou wilt feel truer joy than can
be found in carnal wedlock. Strive, then, to love

me alone; to have me as thy one counsellor, leader, friend, companion, and comrade in all things. And whenever thou speakest to me, say, 'I only and thou, oh, my Lord!' Thou needest not heed any third one. Cling but to me, gaze at me, converse sweetly with me, embrace me, kiss me; expect also all things from me.

(Christ should be considered our only Gain.)

4. "Thou hast seen in other conditions how the men who seek gain busy themselves with endless labours, what artifices they employ, what perils they risk. Thou must now consider all this striving as vanity, knowing that one thing alone is necessary, the grace of God. Therefore, limiting thyself to the one calling which I have entrusted to thee, conduct thy labours faithfully, conscientiously, quietly, entrusting to me the end and aim of all things.

(The Pilgrim is taught to know Christ Himself—the Bible.)

5. "Thou hast seen, when among the scholars, how they strive to fathom all things. Let it be the summit of thy learning to seek me in my works, and to see how wondrously I rule thee and everything. Here wilt thou find more matter for reflection than those yonder,[1] and it will be

---

[1] *I.e.*, those of the world.

with unspeakable delight. Instead of all libraries, to read which is endless labour, with little use and often with harm, while there is always weariness and anxiety, I will give thee this little book in which thou wilt find all arts. Here thy grammar will be to consider my words, thy dialectics faith in them, thy rhetoric prayers and sighs, thy physic meditation on my works, thy metaphysics delight in me and in the eternal things ; thy mathematics will consist in the weighing and measuring of my benefactions, and, on the other hand, of the ingratitude of the world ; thy ethics will be love of me, which will give thee all instructions concerning thy conduct both towards me and towards thy fellow-creatures. But thou must seek all this learning, not that thou mayest please others, but that thou mayest come nearer to me. And in all these things, the simpler thou art, the more learned shalt thou be ; for my light inflames simple hearts.

(We must consider Christ Himself our best Leech.)

6. " Hast thou seen how the leeches contrive divers remedies to defend and prolong life ? But for what purpose shouldst thou trouble about the length of thy life ? Does it, then, depend on thee ? Thou didst not come into the world when thou didst wish it, and thou wilt not leave it when thou wishest, for my providence decides this. Consider, therefore, how thou canst live well, and I will consider how long thou shalt live. Live simply and uprightly according to my pleasure, and I

shall find pleasure in being thy leech for thy good; for I will be thy life, and the length of thy days. Without me, indeed, medicine also is poison; but if I decree it, poison also must become medicine. Therefore, entrust thy life and health to me only, and be thou in perfect peace as to such matters.

(The Pilgrim holds Christ to be his Counsellor, Guide, and Protector.)

7. "In jurisprudence thou hast witnessed the wondrous and entangled intrigues of men, and how they dispute over their divers affairs. But this shall be thy knowledge of law: not to envy any man either the property of others or his own; to leave everyone what he has; not to refuse to any man that which he requires; to give to each one that which thou owest, and even beyond that, as much as thou canst; to be conciliant in all for the sake of peace. If one takes away thy coat, give him thy cloak also; if one strikes thee on one cheek, put forth the other also. These are my laws, and if thou heedest them, thou wilt secure peace.

(What the Religion of Christ is.)

8. "Thou hast seen in the world how men imagine vain ceremonies and strife while performing their religious duties. Thy religion shall be to serve me in quiet, and not to bind thyself by any ceremonies, for I do not bind thee by them. If thou wilt—

according to my teaching—serve me in the spirit and in the truth, then wrangle no further on these matters with any man, even if men call thee a hypocrite, heretic, or I know not what. Cling quietly to me only and to my service.

(*The Government of Christ's Kingdom.*)

9. "While among the great and the rulers of human society, thou hast seen how readily men strive to reach the highest places and to rule over the others. But thou, my son, shalt, as long as thou livest, ever seek the lowest place, and desire to obey, rather than to command. For truly it is easier and safer, and more convenient, to be under others than on the heights. But if thou must yet rule and command, then rule thy own self. I give thee thy soul and body to rule as a kingdom. As many limbs as thou hast in thy body, and divers emotions in thy soul, so many subjects shalt thou have ; see that thy rule over them be good. And should it please my providence to confide to thee yet other tasks, then fulfil them obediently and faithfully, heeding not thy own fancies, but my call.

(*The True Christian's Wars.*)

10. "In the estate of the warriors, thou hast seen that destroying and plundering fellow-men is there considered heroism. But I will tell thee of other enemies against whom thou must henceforth prove thy valour: the devil, the world, and the desires

of thine own body. Guard thyself against these
as well as thou canst, driving from thee the two first,
striking down and killing the third. And when
thou hast bravely done this, thou wilt, I promise,
verily obtain a crown more glorious than those that
the world hath.

(In Christ alone there is Abundance of all.)

11. "Thou hast seen also what the men in that
castle of feigned fortune seek, and in what they
glory: riches, pleasure, fame. Heed thou none of
these things. They give not peace but disquietude,
and they are but the path that leadeth to sorrow.
Wherefore shouldst thou value a multitude of
goods; why desire it? Life requires but little, and
it is my business to provide for those who serve
me. Strive, therefore, to collect inward treasures,
illumination and piety, and I will grant thee
everything else. Heaven and earth will belong to
thee by inheritance; be thou certain of this.
Neither will such things vex thee and oppress thee
as do the things of the world; rather will they give
thee unspeakable joy.

(The Pilgrim's most dear Companions.)

12. "The worldly ones gladly seek companionship; but thou must absent thyself from noisy
striving, and learn to love solitude. Companionship
is but an aid to sin, or to senseless fooling, idleness, or waste of time. Yet wilt thou not be alone;

T

fear not, even if thou art alone. I am with thee, and the multitude of my angels ; with us wilt thou be able to imparl. Yet if at times thou desirest visible companionship also, seek out those who are of the same spirit. Thus will your companionship be a joint devotion to God.

(*True Delights.*)

13. "These others find their pleasure in plentiful banquets, eating, drinking, laughter. But it shall be thy pleasure, when necessary, to hunger, thirst, cry, suffer blows, and so forth, for my sake and with me. Yet if I grant thee pleasurable things, thou mayest also rejoice (but not because of these things, rather because of me, and for my sake).

(*True Glory.*)

14. "Thou hast seen how these others strive for glory and honours ; but thou must not heed the reports of men. Whether men speak well or evil of thee, it imports not, if but I am satisfied with thee. If thou but knowest that thou pleasest me, curry not favour with men ; their good will is fickle, imperfect, perverse ; they often love that which is worthy of hate, and hate that which is worthy of love. Nor is it possible to please all ; striving to please one, thou disgusteth others. By not considering all these, and by heeding me only, thou wilt fare best. If we both then agree together, the voice of man can neither take anything from you

nor from me, nor grant anything. Strive not to
know many, my son. Let thy glory be to be
humble, that the world may, if possible, know
nothing of thee; this is best and safest. My angels,
indeed, will know of thee, speak of thee, seek to
serve thee; announce, if necessary, thy works to
heaven and earth. Be then certain of this. But
truly when the time of the amendment of all
things comes, all ye who have submitted yourselves
to me shalt be led to unspeakable glory before the
angels and the whole world. Compared to this
glory, all worldly glory is but a shadow.

(This is the Summit of all.)

15. "Therefore, my son, I will say briefly: If thou
hast goods, learning, beauty, wit, favour among the
people, and everything that in the world is called
prosperity, be not too proud; if thou hast not
these things, heed it not; forsaking all these things,
whether they be with thee or with others, find thy
inward employment with me. And then having
freed thyself from all created beings, denied also
and renounced thy own self, thou wilt find me, and
in me the fulness of peace; this I promise thee."

*(To give yourself up wholly to Christ is the most
blessed thing.)*

16. And I said: "Lord, my God, I understand
that Thou alone art everything. He who hath
Thee can easily lack the whole world, for in Thee

alone he hath more than he can desire. I erred— I now understand it—when I wandered through the world seeking solace in created things. But from this hour I will delight in naught but in Thee. To thee I now already give myself up wholly. Deign, then, to strengthen me, that I may not abandon Thee in favour of created things, nor again commit the follies of which the world is full. May Thy grace preserve me! I put my full trust in it."

CHAPTER XL

THE PILGRIM IS AS ONE TRANSFORMED

WHILE I speak thus, it appears to me as if there were a strange light around me. The small pictures that I had previously seen partly effaced and broken, I now beheld intact, clear, and beautiful; for thus did they now appear to move before mine eyes. The scattered and broken wheels also were joined together, and out of them was formed a noble instrument similar to a clock, which showed the course of the world, and God's wondrous guidance. The ladders also had been repaired and placed against the windows, through which the heavenly light penetrated, so that—as I understood —one could look outward. The wings, also, that I had seen with plucked plumes had received a new large plumage, and He who was speaking to me— our Lord—took them and fastened them on to me, and said: "My son, I dwell in two spots, in heaven in my glory, and on earth in the hearts of the humble. And I desire that henceforth thou also shouldst have two dwelling-places, one here at home, where I have promised to be with thee; the other with me in heaven. That thou mayest raise thyself thither, I give thee these wings (which are the desire of eternal happines and prayer). If thou dost will it, thou shalt be able to fly upward unto me, and thou shalt have delight in me, and I in thee."

CHAPTER XLI

(New Bridles and Spectacles.)

"MEANWHILE, to strengthen thee in this, and that
thou mayest truly understand the joy to which I
have now called thee, I will send thee among my
other servants, who have already forsaken the
world and given themselves up to me, that thou
mayest behold their ways." "And where, O my
Lord," quoth I, "shall I find them?" He answered:
"They dwell in the world dispersed among the
others, but the world knows them not. But that
thou mayest know them, and also that thou mayest
be safe from the deceits of this world, in which,
till I call thee to me, thou wilt dwell, I will, in
place of the glasses and bridle which thou borest
before, lay on thee my yoke (which is obedience
to me), that thou mayest henceforth follow none
but me. And I will give thee also these spectacles.
If thou gazest through them carefully, thou wilt
be enabled to see better both the vanities of the
world and the delights of my chosen." (Now the
outward border of these spectacles was the Word

of God, and the glass within it was the Holy Ghost.) "Go now," He said: "go to that spot that thou didst pass by before, and thou wilt behold things that, without these aids, thou couldst not have beheld."

(The True Christians in the midst of the Pretended Ones, and wherein they differ.)

2. And now, remembering where I had gone astray before, I arise and go forth eagerly and in haste; thus, though the tumult of the world surrounded me, I now no longer perceived it. I then enter a church that was named "Christianity," and then, seeing in its innermost part, that was the chancel, what seemed a curtain or screen, I immediately approach it, heeding not those sectarians who were wrangling in the aisles. Then only I duly understand what this spot was—to wit, "Praxis Christianismi"[1]; that is, "the truth of Christianity." Now, this screen was two-fold; the outer screen, that appeared but indistinctly, was of dark colour, and was named "Contemptus Mundi"—contempt of the world; the second innermost one was "Amor Christi"—the love of Christ. By these two screens, as I saw, this spot was separated and divided from the others. He, however, who has passed through the innermost portal incontinent becomes somewhat different from other men; he is full of bliss, joy, and peace.

[1] I have here, as elsewhere, transcribed Komensky's Latin quotations verbatim, and given his own translation.

(*There are but few True Christians, and wherefore?*)

3. Then I, standing yet outside and gazing, witness a wondrous and astounding thing: many thousands of men passed by the sanctuary, but did not enter it. Whether they saw it not, or merely heeded it not, or whether, viewed from outside, it appeared evil to them, I know not. I saw also that many who were learned in Scripture—priests, bishops, and others who thought highly of their holiness—went around the sanctuary; some, indeed, looked in, but did not enter; and this appeared mournful to me. I saw also that when one came somewhat nearer, a light flashed on him through a crevice, or a sweet fragrance was wafted towards him, so that he could but seek how to arrive at this spot. But even of those who began to seek the door and look around them, many turned back when the flash of the world again struck them.

(*The Necessity of New Birth.*)

4. But the truest reason why so few arrived there was, as I saw when stepping close to the screen, the very severe examination which they underwent there. For he who desired to enter there had to forsake all his goods, his eyes and ears, his mind and heart; for it was said that he who would be wise before God must become simple of mind; he who wished to know God must forget

everything else; he who wished to possess God must desert everything else. Therefore, some who would not forsake their goods and their learning, contending that such things are helpful to heaven, remained outside and entered not. I saw also that they not only examined the garments of those that were admitted, whether somewhat of earthly vanity was not hidden therein, but they also (a thing unusual elsewhere) took asunder their heads and hearts, that nothing unclean to God might defile His dwelling. This could not, indeed, be done without pain, but by means of heavenly medicine it was done so successfully that it increased rather than diminished the vital power; for in the place of the blood that streamed forth in consequence of the pricking and cutting, a fire was kindled in their limbs which transformed a man into a different one. Then such a man wondered within his mind why he had hitherto loaded himself with such useless burdens, such as the things the world calls wisdom, glory, pleasure, riches; and verily they are but burdens. Here I beheld how the lame skipped, the stammerers spoke eloquently, dull men confounded philosophers, those who had nothing declared that they possessed everything.

(*The Church is the Contrary of the World.*)

5. Seeing this from the entrance, I now went farther beyond the screen and viewed all things— first those that were common to all, then those that belonged to the divers callings—with unspeakable

delight. I see here that everything was contrary to the ways of the world. In the world I beheld everywhere blindness and darkness, here clear light; in the world deceit, here truth; in the world everything was full of disorders, here there was the purest order; in the world I had seen struggling; in the world care and grief, here joy; in the world want, here abundance; in the world slavery and bondage, here freedom; in the world everything was hard and heavy, here everything was easy; in the world there were dangers everywhere, here there was sheer safety. Of this will I narrate somewhat more fully.

CHAPTER XLII

THE LIGHT OF THE INWARD CHRISTIANS

(The Twofold Light of the True Christians.)

THE world and he who struggles in it is ever guided by public opinion; the one clings to the other with regard to their conduct, and they pick their way fumbling as blind men, stopping short and stumbling now here, now there. Yet there dawns on these a twofold clear inward light—the light of reason and the light of faith—and both these are guided by the Holy Ghost.

(The Light of Reason.)

2. For although those who enter must put away and renounce their reason, yet the Holy Ghost returns it to them, purified and refined, so that they are, as it were, full of eyes; wherever they go in the world, whatever they see, hear, smell, taste above them, under them, around them, everywhere they see the footsteps of God, and they know how to turn everything to piety. Therein are they wiser than the wisest philosophers of the world, whom by just judgment God blinds, so that though vainly imagining that they know everything, they

know nothing ; neither what they have nor what
they have not ; neither what they do, nor what—
though it were their duty—they do not, nor to
what purpose they go hither and thither, can they
conceive. Their learning is but on the surface,
mere gaping from outside ; to the innermost
kernel, which is God's glory poured forth everywhere, they do not penetrate. But the Christian
in everything that he sees, hears, touches, smells,
tastes—sees, hears, touches, smells, tastes God ; for
he is certain in his mind that all this is clear truth,
not vain fancy.

(*The Light of Faith.*)

3. Then the light of faith gleams on him so
brightly that he can already see and know, not
only that which is before him, but also everything
that is absent and invisible. In His work, God has
truly revealed that which is on high, above the
heavens, and in the abyss beneath the earth, as
well as what was before the world, and what will
be after it. The Christian, believing in this, has
all this clearly before his eyes, though the world
does not conceive it. The world will believe but
in that which it sees, touches, holds in its hand.
The Christian, on the other hand, is so wholly absorbed in invisible, absent, future things that those
that are before him disgust him. The world ever
demands proof ; the Christian thinks the Word of
God alone sufficient. The world seeks bonds,
pledges, pawns, seals ; the Christian sets up faith

alone as a security for all things. The world examines things for her own purpose in divers fashions, distrusts, tests, suspects. The Christian relies fully on the truthfulness of God. And whereas the world will ever cavil, doubt, question, feel uncertain, the Christian hath ever Him in whom he can place his entire confidence, whom he can obey, and before whom he can humble himself; therefore the light of faith gleams on him, and he can see and know what things are unchangeable, and must be so, even though he cannot grasp them by the light of reason.

(*The Wonders of God seen in this Light. The Course of the World.*)

4. And looking at this light, I behold wondrous, most wondrous, things—more than I dare tell. Yet I will say somewhat. I beheld the world before me as a vast clock-work, fashioned out of divers visible and invisible materials; and it was wholly glassy, transparent and fragile. It had thousands, nay, thousands of thousands, of larger and smaller columns, wheels, hooks, teeth, dents; and all these moved and worked together, some silently, some with much rustling and rattling of divers fashions. In the middle of all stood the largest, principal, yet invisible wheel; from it the various motions of the others proceeded in some unfathomable manner. For the power of the wheel penetrated through all things, and directed everything. How this was done, I was not, indeed, able fully to fathom; but

that it was truly done, I saw very clearly and
evidently. Now, this appeared to me both wondrous
and most delightful: though all these wheels shook
continually, and sometimes vanished for a time—
for the teeth and dents, and even the wheels and
little columns, were sometimes displaced and fell to
pieces—yet the general movement never stopped;
for by some wondrous contrivance of this secret
direction all that was wanting was ever replaced,
filled up, renewed.

(*How Everything is ruled by the Secret Ordinance of God.*)

5. I will speak more clearly: I saw the glory of
God, and how heaven and earth, and the abyss, and
all that can be imagined beyond the world as far
as the endless limits of eternity, were full of His
power and divinity. I saw, say I, how His omni-
potence penetrated everything, and was the foundation of all things; that all that befell in the whole
wide world was according to His will, the smallest
things and the greatest; that also I saw.

(*Particularly among Men.*[1])

6. And, that I may speak of men generally, I
saw how all, both good and bad, live only in God
and with God, thus only move and remain in
existence, and how all their every movements
and breath comes from God and by means of

[1] This refers to the heading of the previous paragraph.

His power. I saw also how His seven eyes—
each one a thousand times brighter than the
sun—penetrate the whole earth, see everything
that befalls in the light or in darkness, openly or
secretly, and even in the deepest depths, watching
thus over the hearts of men. I saw also how His
mercy was poured out on all His creation, and, of
all, most wondrously on men. For I saw how He
loved all, sought their welfare, suffered the sinners,
pardoned the transgressors, called to Him those who
went astray, received those who returned to Him,
waited for those who tarried, spared the stubborn ones, overlooked those who offended Him,
pardoned the contrite, embraced those who humbled
themselves, taught the ignorant, comforted the sor-
rowful, warned men from falling, raised up those
who had fallen, gave to those who implored Him,
granted gifts even to those who implored Him not,
opened to those who knocked, went Himself to
visit those who did not knock, allowed those who
sought Him to find Him, appeared Himself to those
who sought Him not.

(*He is the Terror of the Evil.*)

7. But I saw also His awful and terrible rage
against the stubborn and ungrateful, and how His
wrath pursued and overtook them whitherward
they might go ; thus was it impossible to escape
from His hands, and terrible to fall into them. All
God's subjects, indeed, saw how the awfulness and
majesty of God rules everything, and how, according
to His will only, all great and small things befall.

CHAPTER XLIII

THE LIBERTY OF THOSE HEARTS THAT ARE DEVOTED TO GOD

(*The True Christians are unmoved.*)

THEY obtain, therefore, that for which all the wisest men in the world have laboured vainly—to wit, full liberty of the mind; hence are they subject and bound to nothing but to God, nor are they obliged to do anything contrary to their will. In the world, as I had seen, everything was full of disappointment; the business of each man went differently from what he wished. Everyone was dependent on himself or others more than was beseeming, and being forcibly carried along by his own will or that of others, he ever warred either with himself or with others. Here everything was calm. For each one of these men had given himself over wholly to God, heeded nothing else, recognised no one save God as being above him. Therefore they obeyed not the commands of the world, flung its promises from them, laughed at its threats; everything outward they declared evil, for they were certain of their inward treasure.

(The True Christians are unyielding.)

2. Therefore the true Christian, who otherwise is yielding, cordial, willing, and ready to render service, is unyielding as regards the privilege of his heart. Therefore he values neither his friends nor his foes, nor his lord, nor his king, nor his wife, nor his children, nor lastly himself, so highly that for the sake of any of these he would abandon his purpose—to wit, his fear of God; rather does he walk everywhere with straight step. Whatever the world around him may do, say, threaten, promise, advise, beg, counsel, urge, he does not allow himself to be moved by any of these things.

(The Greatest Freedom and also the Greatest Bondage.)

3. As the world is ever perverse, and catches at the shadow rather than at the truth, so doth it here also; it founds its liberty on this, that he who is free should grant nothing to others, and should give himself over to sloth, pride, or passion. But the conduct of the Christian is far different. Only guarding his heart well that he may in freedom preserve it for God alone, he employs everything else for the wants of his fellow-men. Thus did I see and understand that no one in the world is more ready to serve than a man who is devoted to God. He gladly and willingly undertakes to render even such humble services of which he

whom the world has intoxicated would be ashamed. If he but sees what can benefit a fellow-man, he does not hesitate, does not delay, spares no trouble, does not extol the services he has rendered, nor reproachfully remind others of them; whether he meets with gratitude or ingratitude, he continues serving quietly and gaily.

(And what a Fair Thing this is.)

4. Oh, blessed servitude of the sons of God, than which nothing freer can be imagined—a servitude in which he submits himself to God alone, that he may otherwise be free in everything ! Oh, unhappy freedom of the world, than which nothing can be more slavish, wherein man, heeding not God Himself, wretchedly consents to become the slave of others, namely, when he serves created beings, over whom he should rule, and resists God, whom he should obey. Oh, mortals, did we but understand that there is One, One only, over us—the Lord our Creator and future Judge ! He alone has the power to give us commands ; but He commands us not as slaves, but as children who should obey Him. Free and unfettered He wishes us to be, even when we obey Him. Verily, to serve Christ is to be as a king ; for to be God's serf is a far greater glory than to be the monarch of the whole world. What, then, must it be to be God's friend and child ?

CHAPTER XLIV

THE REGULATIONS OF THE INWARD CHRISTIANS

(*God's Laws are brief.*)

FREE, indeed, the Lord God wishes His children to be, but not wilful. Therefore has He hedged them in by certain regulations in a fashion better and more perfect than anything that I had ever beheld in the world. There everything was full of disorder, partly because they had no certain rules, partly because, as I saw, even when they had rules they did not heed them. But those who dwelt behind the curtain had most noble rules, and also obeyed them. They have, indeed, laws given by God Himself that are full of justice, and by which it is decreed: 1. That everyone who is devoted to God should acknowledge and know Him as the only God. 2. That he should serve Him in the spirit and in the truth without vainly imagining corporal things. 3. He should use his tongue, not for the purpose of offence, but for the glorification of God's holy name. 4. The times and hours that are ordained for God's service he shall employ for nothing but His inward and outward service. 5. He shall obey his parents and others whom God has placed over him. 6. He shall not injure the life of his fellow-men. 7. He shall preserve the purity of his body. 8. He shall not seize the property of others. 9. He shall beware of falsehood and deceit. 10. And lastly, he shall maintain his mind within barriers and the ordained boundaries.

(*A Summing-up in Two Words.*)

2. The summa of everything is that everyone should love God above all things that can be named, and that he should sincerely wish well to his fellow-men, as to himself. And this summing-up of the contents of God's Word was, as I heard, greatly praised ; indeed, I myself found and felt that it was more valuable than the countless worldly laws, rules, and decrees, for it was a thousand times more perfect.

(*The True Christian requires not Copious Laws.*)

3. To him who verily loves God with his whole heart, it is not necessary to give many commandments as to when, where, how, and how often he should serve God, worship and honour Him ; for his hearty union with God, and his readiness to obey Him is the fashion in which he honours God best, and it leads a man to ever and everywhere praise God in his mind, and to strive for His glory in all his deeds. He also who loves his fellow-men as himself requires not copious commandments as

to where, when, and wherein he should serve them, how he should avoid to injure them, and return to them what is due to them. This love for his fellow-men will in itself tell him fully, and show him how he should bear himself towards them. It is the sign of the evil man that he always demands rules, and wishes to know only from the books of law what he should do ; yet at home in our heart God's finger shows us that it is our duty to do unto our neighbours that which we wish that they should do unto us. But as the world cares not for this inward testimony of our own conscience, but heeds external laws only, therefore is there no true order in the world ; there is but suspicion, distrust, misunderstanding, ill-will, discord, envy, theft, murder, and so forth. Those who are truly subject to God heed but their own conscience ; what it forbids them they do not, but they do that which it tells them they may do ; of gain, favour, and such things they take no care.

(*There is Unanimity among True Christians.*)

4. There is therefore equality among them, and great similitude also, as if they had all been cast in one mould ; all think the same things, believe the same things, all like and dislike the same things, for all are taught by one and the same spirit.

And it is worthy of wonder that—as I here saw with pleasure—men who had never seen each other, heard each other, and who were separated by the whole world, were quite similar the one to

the other ; for as if one had been in the body of
the other, they spoke alike, saw alike, felt alike.
Thus, though there was a great variety in their
gifts, just as on a musical instrument the sound of
the strings or pipes differs, and is now weaker, now
stronger, yet a delightful harmony resounded
among them. This is the purpose of the Christian
unity,[1] and the foretoken of eternity, when
everything will be done in one spirit.

(Sympathy among True Christians.)

5. From this equality sympathy among them
arises ; thus all rejoiced with those who rejoiced,
were doleful with those who had dole. I had in
the world seen a most evil thing that had
grieved me not once: if one fared ill, the others
rejoiced ; if he erred, the others laughed ; if he
suffered injury, the others sought gain therefrom ;
indeed, for the sake of their own gain, pleasure,
and amusement, they themselves led a fellow-man
to his downfall and injury.

But among the holy men I found everything
otherwise ; for every man strove as bravely and as
diligently to avert unhappiness and discomfort
from his neighbours as from himself. Could he
not avert it, he grieved not otherwise than if the
misfortune had befallen himself, and he grieved
because all were one heart, one soul. As the iron
needles of a compass, when once they have been

---

[1] Komensky here obviously alludes to the religious
community to which he belonged.

touched by the magnet-stone, all point to one and
the same direction of the world, so the souls of all
these men, touched by the spirit of love, all turn to
one and the same direction; in case of happiness
to joy, in case of unhappiness to dole. And here
also did I understand that those are false Christians who indeed busy themselves carefully with
their own matters, but care not for those of their
neighbours. They steadfastly turn aside from the
hand of God, and preserving carefully their own
nest, they leave the others outside in the wind and
rain. But different, far different, I found things
here. If one suffered, the others did not rejoice;
if one hungered, the others did not feast; if one
was warring, the others did not sleep; everything
was done in common, and it was delightful to
behold this.

(*There is Community in all Good Things among the True Christians.*)

6. As regards possessions, I saw that, though
most of them were poor, had but little of the things
the world calls treasures, and cared but little for
them, yet almost everyone had something that was
his own. But he did not hide this, nor conceal it
from the others (as is the world's way); he held it
as in common, readily and gladly granting and
lending it to him who might require it. Thus
they all dealt with their possessions not otherwise
than those who sit together at one table deal with
the utensils of the table, which all use with equal

right. Seeing this, I thought with shame that with us everything befalls in contrary fashion. Some fill and overfill their houses with utensils, clothing, food, gold, and silver, as much as they can; meanwhile others, who are equally servants of God, have hardly wherewith to clothe and feed themselves. But, I must say, I understood that this was by no means the will of God; rather is it the way of the world, the perverse world, that some should go forth in festive attire, others naked; that some should belch from overfilling, while others yawn from hunger; some should laboriously earn silver, some vainly squander it; some make merry, others wail. Thence there sprung up among the one, pride and contempt of the others; and among these again, fury, hatred, and misdeeds. But here there was nothing such. All were in community with all; indeed, their souls also.

(*There is Intimacy among True Christians.*)

7. Therefore is there great intimacy among them, openness, and holy companionship; therefore all, however different their gifts and their callings may be, consider and hold themselves as brethren; for they say that we have all sprung from the same blood, have been redeemed and cleansed by the same blood, that we are children of one Father, approach the same table,[1] await the same inheritance in heaven, and so forth. Except as regards non-essential matters, one man hath not more than

[1] *I.e.*, at Communion.

another. Therefore I saw that they surpassed each other in kindness and modesty, gladly served one another, and each one employed his own powers for the benefit of the others. He who had judgment counselled ; he who had learning taught ; he who had strength defended the others ; he who had power maintained order among them. If one erred in some things, they admonished him ; if he sinned, they punished him ; and each one gladly accepted admonition and punishment, and was ready to amend everything according to what was told him, and even to forfeit his life when it was shown to him that it was not his own.[1]

[1] *I.e.*, that it belonged to God.

CHAPTER XLV

(It is easy to obey God.)

NOR is it bitter to them to conform to such orders, rather is it their pleasure and delight, while I had seen in the world that each man did unwillingly what he had to do. Verily, God had deprived these men of their stony hearts, and placed in their bodies fleshly pliant ones that were obedient to the will of God. The devil, indeed, with his crafty suggestions, the world with its scandalous examples, the body with its innate tardiness on the right path, troubled them much. But this they heeded not. They drove away the devil by the artillery of their prayers; they guarded themselves against the world by the shield of resolute will; they compelled their bodies to obedience by the scourge of discipline. Thus did they joyfully perform their duties, and the spirit of Christ that dwelt with them gave them such strength that they were wanting neither in goodwill nor in good deeds (within the limits of earthly perfection). Here, then, did I truly see that to serve God with your whole heart is not labour, but joy, and I understood that those who lay too much stress on the weakness of man do not understand the strength and value of their new birth, and have, indeed, perhaps not attained it. Let them then take heed of this. I saw not that anyone among them claimed absolution from his sins because of the weakness of the flesh, or excused his evil deeds by the frailness of his nature. Rather did I see that if a man had devoted his whole heart to his Creator, who had redeemed him, and consecrated his body as a temple, then following his heart, his other limbs also freely and gradually took that direction to which God willed them. Oh, Christian, whoever and wherever thou art, free thyself from the fetters of flesh! See, know, and understand that the obstacles which thou imaginest in thy mind are far too small that they could impede thy will, if it be but sincere.

2. I saw also that not only to do what God commands, but also to suffer what God imposes, is easy. Here no few were slapped, spat on, whipped by the worldly ones; yet they rejoiced, and lifting their hands heavenward, praised God that He had thought them worthy of suffering somewhat for His sake; for not only did they believe in Him who was crucified, but they also, they said, were crucified for His sake. Some who fared not thus envied the others with holy envy, fearing God's wrath if they received no correction, and separation from Christ if they had no cross. Therefore they kissed the rod and stick of God

whenever they touched them, and gratefully took His cross upon them.

3. Now, all this sprang from their complete subjection to the will of God; thus they desired to do nothing, to be nothing, but what God wished. Therefore are they certain that whatever befalls them comes to them from God, according to His prudent consideration. Nothing unexpected can, indeed, befall such men; for they count wounds, prison torture, and death among God's gifts. To live joyfully or dolefully is indifferent to them, except that they consider the former more dangerous, the latter safer. Therefore they delight in their troubles, wounds and stripes, and are proud of them. In all things they are so hardy in God's faith, that if they suffer not somewhat, they imagine that they are idling and losing time. But let all hold their hands aloof from these men; the more willingly they offer their back to the stripes, the more difficult it is to strike them; the more similar they are to fools, the more dangerous it is to mock them. For they are not their own masters, but belong to God; and all that is done unto them God considers as done unto Himself.

CHAPTER XLVI

THE HOLY ONES HAVE ABUNDANCE OF EVERYTHING

(To be Content with what a Man has is True Wealth.)

THE world is full of Marthas, who run and
wander to and fro, toil, and scrape silver together
from all directions, and yet never have enough.
But these holy men have a different nature; each of
them sits quietly at the feet of his Lord, and this, and
what he receives therethrough, is sufficient to him.
He holds the grace of God that resides within him
as the most precious treasure; in this alone he finds
delight; external things which the world calls riches
he considers as a burden rather than a gain, yet
they use them for the necessities of life—for the
necessities only, I say. Therefore, whether the
Lord God grants each of them little or much, each
of them says that he has enough. They verily
believe, and put their trust therein, that they are
under God's protection, and therefore think it
unseemly to desire anything beyond that which
God has granted them.

2. Now I beheld here a wondrous thing. There
were some among these holy men who had an

ample supply of riches, silver, gold crowns, and sceptres (for there are such men also among God's chosen); others had scarcely anything beyond a half-naked body, that was dried up by hunger and thirst. Yet the former said they had nothing, and the latter said they had everything, and both were of good cheer. And then I understood that he is truly rich and in want of nothing who knows how to be content with that which he has. To have a large, a small, or no house, costly, poor, or no clothing, many friends or one, or none, high rank, low rank, or no rank, to have or not to have rank or office or glory, generally to be something or to be nothing, is to them one and the same thing; for as man must believe that to go, to stand, to sit wherever God leads, or places, or seats him is the only truly good thing, better even than man can imagine.

3. Oh, blessed and most desirable abundance! How happy are those who are rich in this fashion! For though some may appear wretched and miserable in the eyes of the world, yet are they a thousand times better provided, even as regards external things, than the rich men of the world; for these who are their own purveyors are, with their goods, exposed to thousands of accidents; fire, water, rust, theft, and so forth may deprive them of them. But the holy men who have God as their purveyor ever find with Him an inexhaustible store for all their wants. He daily feeds them from His store-rooms, clothes them from His chamber, gives them from His treasury that which they require

for their expenditure; not, indeed, in great abundance, but all that is seemly and sufficient. He does this not according to the minds of men, but according to His providence, on which they rely a thousand times more readily than on their minds.

CHAPTER XLVII

THE SAFETY OF THOSE WHO ARE DEVOTED TO GOD

(*The Angels as Guardians.*)

Now nothing in the world appeared so exposed and subject to divers dangers than the band of the godly, at which the devil and the world looked angrily, menacing to strike and smite them. Yet I saw that they were well sheltered; for I saw that their whole community was encompassed by a wall of fire. When I came nearer I saw that this wall moved, for it was nothing else but a procession of thousands and thousands of angels who walked around them; no foe, therefore, could approach them. Each one of them also had an angel who had been given to him by God and ordained to be his guardian, that he might guard him and preserve him, and protect him against all dangers and snares, pits, ambushes, traps, and temptations. They are, no doubt (I understood and saw this), the friends of the men who are their fellow-servants, and watch them that they may uphold the duties for which they were created by God; thus they serve men readily, guard them against the devil, evil folk, and unhappy accidents; and carrying them, if necessary, on their own hands, they shield them from injury. Here, too, I understood how great is the import of godliness ; for these beautiful and pure spirits remained only where they smelt the perfume of virtue, while they were driven away by the stink of sin and uncleanliness.

(*The Angels our Teachers.*)

2. I saw also (and it is not beseeming to conceal this) another advantage of this holy, invisible companionship—to wit, that the angels were not only as guards, but also as teachers to the chosen. They often give them secret knowledge of divers things, and teach them the deep secret mysteries of God. For as they ever behold the countenance of the omniscient God, nothing that a godly man can wish to know can be secret to them, and with God's permission they reveal that which they know, and which it is necessary that the chosen should know. Therefore the heart of the godly often feels that which has befallen elsewhere, mourns with the mournful, and rejoices with the joyful. Therefore, also, can they, by means of dreams and other visions, or of secret inspirations, imagine in their minds that which has befallen, or befalls, or will befall. Thence comes also other increase of the gifts of God within us, deep, valuable meditations, divers wondrous discoveries by means of which man often surpasses himself, though he knows not how he has that power. Oh, blessed school of the sons of God! It is this which often

causes the astonishment of all worldly-wise men, when they see how some plain little fellow speaks wondrous mysteries ; prophesies the future changes in the world and in the Church as if he saw them before his eyes ; mentions the names of yet unborn kings and heads of states ; proclaims and announces other things that could not be conceived either by any study of the stars or by any endeavour of human wit.[1]

We cannot sufficiently thank God, our guardian, for these things, nor love sufficiently these our heavenly teachers. But let us return to the security of the godly.

(*God is the Shield of His own.*)

Then I saw that every one of the godly was protected not only by the guard of angels, but also by the venerable presence of God. Thus terror befell those who, contrary to the will of God, endeavoured to touch them. I saw miracles among some of them, how they were thrown into the water or fire, or as a prey to lions and wild beasts ; yet they suffered no injury. Human fury attacked some of them shamefully. Bands of tyrants and hangmen, with countless followers, surrounded them. Sometimes powerful kings and whole kingdoms strove unto exhaustion to destroy them.

[1] This is an allusion to the so-called prophecies of Kotter, Ponatovská and Drabík. I have referred to them in my "History of Bohemian Literature," pp. 256-259, and pp. 271-273.

Yet nothing befell them ; they stood together, or went their way merrily, pursuing their callings. And now I understood what it is to have God as a shield, for He entrusts to His servants certain tasks in the world, and they manfully do their duty. He is ever in them and with them, and guards them as the apple of His eye, that they may not die before they accomplish the task for which they were sent into the world.

(*The Holy Boasts of the Godly.*)

4. This, indeed, the godly know, and they cheerfully rely on God's protection. I have heard some of them boast that they were not afraid even should the shadow of death be before them ; even should thousands of thousands be in arms against them ; even should the whole world be enraged, the land be tossed into the middle of the sea, the whole world be full of devils, and so forth. Oh, most happy security, unheard of in the world ! For man, closed up and sheltered in the hand of God, is removed from the influence of all other things. Let us, then, all ye honest servants of Christ, understand that we have a most watchful guardian, protector, defender—the Almighty God Himself. Therefore let us rejoice !

CHAPTER XLVIII

THE GODLY HAVE PEACE ON ALL SIDES

WHILE I had previously seen in the world much unquietude and toil, trouble and care, horror and fear among all estates, I now found much quiet and much goodwill among those who were subject to God ; for they dreaded not God, knowing well how kindly His heart inclined to them. Neither did they find within themselves anything over which they could grieve. Of all good things (as has already been shown) they had no want ; neither felt they any discomfort from the things that surrounded them, for they heeded them not.

(The True Christians heed not the Derision of the World.)

2. Now it is true that the evil world granted them but little rest, and, indeed, did everything it could to spite and mock them ; it grinned at them, bit its thumb at them, pelted them, spat at them, tripped them up, and whatever worse things can be imagined. Of this I saw many examples, and I understood that it befell, according to the orders of God the Highest, that those who wish to be good

325

here must wear cap and bells; for the ways of the world bring it with them that what is wisdom before God is to the world sheer folly. I saw, therefore, that many to whom God had granted His noblest gifts had to endure the contempt and derision of the others, often even of those who were nearest to them. Thus, I say, did it befall; but I saw also that the godly heeded this not, that they, indeed, gloried therein that the worldly stopped up their noses before them as before a stench, averted their eyes from them as from something loathsome, scorned them as fools, put them to death as malefactors. For they said that their watchword, by which it was known that they belonged to Christ, was " not to please the world." They said also that he who knows not how to suffer wrongs gaily hath not yet fully the spirit of Christ; thus spake they of these things, and fortified each other. They also said that the world showed no indulgence likewise to those who belonged to it; indeed, it insulted, deceived, robbed, tormented them; if, then, it wished to do the same with the godly, it was well. " If," said they, " we cannot avoid this torment, we will endure it there, where, for the accidental injuries inflicted by the worldly, we are recompensed by the bountiful, generous kindness of God. Therefore do we consider their derision, injury, and ill-will as our gain."

(*To the True Christian everything* [1] *is indifferent.*)

3. Nay, this also did I understand, that these true Christians would not even hear of the distinctions between what the world calls happiness or unhappiness, riches or poverty, honour or dishonour; for everything, they said, that proceeds from the hand of God is good, happy, and salutary. Nothing, therefore, grieves them; they are never irresolute or reluctant. To command or to obey, to teach others or to be taught by them, to have plenty or to suffer want, is one and the same thing to the true Christian; he proceeds on his way with a calm countenance, striving only to please God. They say that the world is not so heavy that it may not be endured, nor so valuable that its loss need be regretted. Therefore neither the desire for anything nor the loss of anything causes the true Christian suffering. If someone smites him on the right cheek, he cheerfully turns to him the other one also. And if one disputes with him about his cloak, he lets him have his coat also. He leaves everything to God, his witness and judge, and feels assured that all these things will, in the course of time, be revised, amended, and at last justly decided.

[1] *I.e.*, all external things.

(What the True Christian sees outwardly.)

4. Neither does one of God's own allow himself
to be disturbed in the peace of his mind by the
nations of the world.   Many things, indeed,
displease him ; but he does not, therefore, grieve or
sorrow within his mind.   Let that go backward
that will not go straightly forward ; that fall that
cannot stand ; that perish that cannot or will not
endure.   Why should a Christian grieve for this
whose conscience is righteous, and who has in his
heart the love of God ?   If men will not conform to
our customs, let us then conform to theirs ; at least,
as far as our conscience permits it.   The world, it
is true, is going from bad to worse, but by our
fretting shall we improve it ?

*(The True Christian heedeth not the Tumult of the
World.)*

5. The mighty of the world rage and dispute
about crowns and sceptres ; thence arise devastations
of lands and countries ; but this also the enlightened Christian heeds not greatly within his mind.
He thinks that it is of little or no import who
rules the world ; for the world, even should Satan
himself hold its sceptre, cannot destroy the Church.
On the other hand, if a crowned angel ruled it, it
would yet remain the world, and those who desire
to be truly godly would yet have to suffer.   It
therefore appears indifferent to them who sits on

the throne of the world; indeed, if one of the godly
sits on it (and experience has proved this), many
flatterers and hypocrites mix with the band of the
godly, and through this admixture the piety of the
others also cools ; and, on the other hand, in time of
open persecution only the godly serve God, and
with full ardour. It must also be considered that
in such circumstances [1] many conceal themselves
under the covering of the common welfare, piety,
honesty, privileges; but could we look through
them thoroughly, it would be found that they
seek kingdoms, privileges, glory, not for Christ,
but for themselves. Therefore the true Christian
lets all such matters befall, as they can and will.
To him who is alone in the dwelling of his heart,
God and His grace are sufficient.

*(The Godly One also heeds not the Sufferings that
befall the Church.)*

6. Neither do the temptations that surround the
Church trouble an enlightened soul. The godly know
that triumph will at last be theirs. They know
also that they cannot obtain it without a victory,
nor obtain a victory without fighting, nor a fight
without foes and hard conflict with them. They
therefore bravely endure what may befall them or
others ; for they are certain that victory is God's,
who will guide all things whither He designs them ;
be it even that rocks, mountains, a sea or abyss

[1] *I.e.*, under the rule of a godly prince.

be in the way, yet must they at last disappear.
They know also that all this raging of God's foes
against Him can but increase the glory of His
name.   For if some matter begun for God's glory
had met with no resistance, it might be thought
that it had been begun by men and carried out by
the force of man.   Now, on the contrary, the more
furious is the resistance of the world and all its
devils, the clearer does the power of God appear.

*(The Sorrows of the Godly can easily be driven
away in a Twofold Fashion.)*

7. Nay, even if such accidents befell them (and
I saw examples of this) that gave them dole within
their minds, yet they endured not long with them,
and soon vanished, as a little cloud before the sun.
For they have a twofold remedy ; one is the
thought of a happy future, which is of greater
value than the troubles of the world, and which
awaits them.   That which befalls here is but
temporary ; it appears and again vanishes, is lost,
disappears ; therefore is it unbeseeming to crave
any of these worldly things much, or to grieve
much at their loss, for such things are but as the
clatter of a moment.   The other remedy of the
godly is that they have ever a guest in their
homes, and if they converse but a little with Him,
they are able to drive away every grief, even the
greatest.   This guest is God, their comforter, to
whom they cling with their whole hearts, and to
whom they narrate familiarly and openly all that

grieves them. They have indeed this brave confidence, that in all their concerns they hasten to appeal to God. Every one of their transgressions, offences, deficiencies, weaknesses, sorrows, strivings, they pour into His fatherly lap, and they entrust themselves to Him in everything. And as the Lord God can but love this filial, kind confidence in Himself, He cannot but grant the godly His consolation, as well as His help that they may bear their suffering. Thus the more their sufferings are renewed and multiplied, the more is God's peace renewed and multiplied within them, and that surpasses all earthly wit.

CHAPTER XLIX

THE GODLY HAVE CONSTANT DELIGHT WITHIN THEIR HEARTS

(*A Good Conscience is an Incessant Feast.*)

THE godly have not only simple peace within them, but also joy and pleasure, which flow to their hearts from the presence and feeling of God's love. For where God is, there is heaven; where heaven is, there is eternal joy, and where there is eternal joy there men desire nothing further. All the joys of the world are but a shade, jest, derision, compared to this joy; only I know not in what words to describe and portray it. I saw, I saw, I saw and understood that to have within you God, with His · celestial treasures, is so glorious a thing that all the glory, splendour, glitter of the world cannot be compared to it. It is a thing so joyful that the whole world could neither take anything from it nor add anything to it, so great and high that the whole world can neither conceive it nor contain it.

(*N.B.*)

2. For how can anything be otherwise than sweet and joyful to a man who possesses this

332

divine light within him through the Spirit of God, such freedom from the world and its slavery, such certain and ample divine protection, such safety from enemies and accidents ; lastly, as has been shown, that feeling of continuous peace ? This is that sweetness that the world understandeth not ; this that sweetness that he who once tasted it strives for at any risk ; this that sweetness from which no other sweetness can separate us, no bitterness drive us away, no other charm entice us away, and from which no bitterness, not even death, can turn us away.

3. And then I understood what sometimes impels many of God's saints to throw from them so willingly honours, favour of the people, their worldly estates. They would be equally ready to cast from them the whole world, if it were theirs. I understood also how others, again, cheerfully gave over their bodies to prison, whip, or death, ready to suffer a thousand deaths, could the world repeat the penalty. Should they perish by means of water or fire, or under the sword of the executioner, they were yet prepared cheerfully to sing hymns. Oh, Lord Jesus, how sweet art Thou to the souls that have tasted of Thee ! Blessed is he who comprehends this delight !

CHAPTER L

THE PILGRIM BEHOLDS THE CHRISTIANS ACCORDING TO THEIR ESTATES

I HAVE till now narrated but the incidents common to all true Christians ; but when I saw that among them also, as among the worldly ones, there were divers callings, I became desirous to witness how they administered their offices. Here, again, I found a most noble order in everything, delightful to behold. I will not fully describe all this ; briefly only will I mention some things.

(What Marriage is among Christians.)

2. Their marriage, I saw, was not widely apart from virginity, for with them there is much moderation both in their desires and in their cares. Instead of those steely fetters, I saw here golden clasps ; instead of endeavours to separate, I saw joyful union both of bodies and of hearts. Then if any hardship yet clung to this estate, it was made good by the multiplication of the subjects of God's kingdom that resulted from it.

(What Magistrates the True Christians have among them.)

3. Now he to whom it befell to sit above the others and be called magistrate behaved thus to the subjects that were entrusted to him as is the manner of parents to their children, that is, kindly and carefully ; and it was delightful to witness this. I saw, also, that many of these magistrates folded their hands and praised God. Then, again, he who was under the rule of another strove to bear himself in such a fashion that he was a subject not only in word but also in deed. He honoured God in this that he showed great respect and attention, both in words and in deeds and thoughts, to him whom He had placed over him, whatever his character might be.

(The Learned Men among the Christians.)

4. When I had proceeded farther among them, I found no few learned men, who, contrary to the customs of the world, surpassed the others in humility as greatly as they did in learning, and they were sheer gentleness and kindness. It befell that I spoke to one of them, from whom it was thought no earthly learning was concealed ; yet he bore himself as a most simple man, sighing deeply over his stupidity and ignorance. The knowledge of languages they held in slight value, if the knowledge of wisdom was not added to it. For

languages, they said, give not wisdom, but have that purpose only that by means of them we can converse with many and divers inhabitants of the terrestrial globe, be they alive or dead. Therefore not he, they said, who can speak many languages, but he who can speak of useful things, is learned. Now they called useful things all God's works, and they said that arts are of some use for the purpose of understanding Him; but they also say that the true fountain of knowledge is the Holy Writ, and the Holy Ghost our teacher, and that the purpose of all true knowledge is Christ, He who was crucified. Therefore, as I saw, all these learned men tended with all their learning to Christ, as to the centre; and everything, they say, that was an obstacle to their approaching Christ they reject, even if it was most learned. I saw also that they read divers human books, according to their pursuits; but the choicest only they read carefully, and they always consider human statements as human only. They write books themselves also, but not to spread their fame among the people, but rather because they hope to impart something useful to their fellow-men, to aid the common welfare, to frustrate the wicked.

(The Priests and Theologians of the True Christians.)

5. Of priests and preachers I saw a certain number among them, according to the wants of the Church; all were in simple attire, and

their ways were gentle and kind. They spent their time more with God than with men, in prayer, reading, and reflection. What time they have besides they employ in teaching others, either generally in the assemblies or separately in private. Their hearers assured me, and I felt it also myself, that no one could listen to their preaching without inward emotion of the heart and the conscience, for the power of divine eloquence came from their lips. I saw also rejoicing and tears among the listeners, when the preachers spoke of the mercy of God, and of the ingratitude of the world; so truthfully, livingly, and fervently did they preach. They would have held it a disgrace to teach others anything wherein they had not already set them an example; therefore one can learn from them, even when they are silent. I approached one of these preachers, wishing to speak to him. He was a man with venerable grey hair, and on his countenance somewhat of the divine incontinently appeared. When he spoke to me, his speech was full of a kindly severity, and it was in every way clear that he was God's ambassador; for he was in no way tainted by the smell of the world. When, as is our custom, I wished to address him according to his rank,[1] he permitted it not, calling such things worldly fooling; it was a sufficient title and honour for him, he said, if I addressed him as "servant of God," or, if I wished it, as "my father." When he gave me his blessing I felt, I know not

---

[1] *I.e.*, as preacher or priest.

what sweetness and joy that arose within my heart, and then I truly understood that true theology is a more powerful and more penetrative thing than we generally imagine. And I blushed, remembering the haughtiness, pride, avarice, the mutual quarrels, the envy, hatred, drunkenness, and carnality of some of our priests; the words and deeds of such men, verily, are so wide apart that they seem to speak as in jest only of the virtues of Christian life. On the other hand, these preachers, that I may speak the truth, pleased me, being men of fervent mind and continent body, men who were lovers of celestial things, but heeded not earthly ones. They were careful of their flock, forgetful of themselves, moderate in wine, though their minds were intoxicated by the spirit of holiness, modest of speech, though plentiful in good deeds; and each one among them strove to be first in work, last in good deeds; in all their deeds, words, and thoughts, they cared but for their spiritual progress.

CHAPTER LI

THE DEATH OF FAITHFUL CHRISTIANS

(Death is pleasant to a Christian.)

Now when I had walked sufficiently among these
Christians and beheld their deeds, I at last found
that Death walked about among them also; but
she was not, as in the world, of morose aspect,
naked, unlovely, but she was folded up in the
grave-clothes of Christ, that He had left in his
sepulchre. She approached now this man, now
that one, telling him that it was time that he
should leave the world. Oh, how great was the
joy and delight of those who received such news!
Only that this should befall sooner, they were
ready to endure all suffering, the sword, fire, pincers,
and every torture. Thus did each of them fall
into his slumber, peacefully, quietly, and gladly.

(What befell after their Death.)

2. Then I, who wished to see what would now
befall them, beheld God's angel, who, according to
His divine command, sought out for each of them
a spot where he was to have his little chamber,

and where his body should have rest. When it had been laid there either by friends or by enemies, or by the angels themselves, they guarded the sepulchre, that the graves of the holy might be preserved safely from Satan, and that not even the smallest atom of the dust within them should be lost. Meanwhile, other angels took the soul, and carried it upward with splendour and divine rejoicing. Then when I put my glasses of faith aright, I gazed upward, and beheld unspeakable glory.

CHAPTER LII

THE PILGRIM BEHOLDS THE GLORY OF GOD

AND behold, the Lord of Hosts sat on His throne on high, and there was splendour around Him from one end of the heavens to the other, and under His feet there was a gleaming as of crystals, emeralds, and sapphires, and His throne was of jasper, and around Him there was a beautiful rainbow. Thousands of thousands and ten times a thousand times a hundred thousand angels stood around Him, singing together: "Holy, holy, holy, Lord of the hosts! Heaven and earth are full of Thy glory."

2. Then twenty-four elders fell on their knees before the throne, laid down their crowns at the feet of Him who lives in all eternity, and sang with a loud voice: "Thou art worthy, O Lord, to receive glory, and honour, and power, for according to Thy will do they abide, and have they been created."

3. I saw also before the throne another great host whom none could count; in it were men of all nations, and races, countries, and tongues; and as the angels carried upward those of God's saints who had died on the earth, the number ever increased, and the sound ever became louder.

They exclaimed : " Amen, blessing and glory, wisdom, gratitude, and honour, power and strength to our God in all eternity ! Amen."

4. Now did I behold splendour, light, magnificence, and unspeakable glory, hear sounds and notes that are inexpressible, witness things that were joyful and more wondrous than our eyes, ears, and heart can conceive.

5. Terrified by the sight of these so glorious heavenly things, I also fell down before the throne of divine majesty, ashamed of my sinfulness, and of being a man of tainted lips, and I exclaimed : " Lord, Lord, Lord, Thou who art a strong God, compassionate, merciful, long-suffering, and plentiful in mercy and justice ! He who grants mercy to thousands, and forgives unrighteousness, trespasses and sin. O Lord ! have mercy on me the sinner also, for the sake of Jesus Christ."

CHAPTER LIII

THE PILGRIM IS RECEIVED INTO GOD'S HOUSEHOLD

WHEN I had spoken thus, my Saviour, the Lord
Jesus Christ, from the centre of His throne, spake
these delightful words: " Be not afeard, my dear
one. I am with thee, thy Redeemer and Comforter,
therefore be not afeard. Thy misdeed has been
taken from thee, and thy sin has been purged.
Rather be glad and rejoice, for thy name is
written down among those of the elect; if thou
servest me faithfully thou wilt be as one of them.
Whatever thou hast seen, use it in fear of me, and
thou wilt behold yet greater things. Be careful of
those things only for which I have called thee, and
walk on that path to glory which I have shown
thee. Abide in the world as long as I leave thee
in it, as a pilgrim, a stranger, a foreigner, a guest;
but remain with me as a member of my household.
I give unto thee the citizenship of heaven. Be
therefore careful in the world. Have a mind that
is—as much as possible—lifted both upward to me
and kindly downward to thy fellow-men. Use,
then, worldly things as long as thou art there, but
rejoice in heavenly ones only. Be compliant to me
only, adverse and refractory to the world and the

flesh. Guard within thee the wisdom that I have granted thee, and outwardly the simplicity that I have counselled thee; have a resounding heart, but a silent tongue. Be tender in thy feeling for the suffering of others, but hardy against the wrong that may befall thee. Serve with thy soul me alone, with thy body him whom thou canst or must. What I order thee thou must do; the burden I lay on thee thou must bear. Be to the world unbending, and cling ever to me. Let thy body be in the world, thy heart with me. If thou wilt but act thus, thou wilt be blessed, and wilt fare well. Proceed, then, my dear son, and remain true to thy calling until thy end, but gladly enjoy the solace to which I have led thee."

CHAPTER LIV

THE END OF ALL

THEN the vision vanished from mine eyes, and
falling on my knees, I raised my eyes upward
towards my Redeemer and thanked Him as well as
I knew, saying :

"Be Thou blessed, my Lord and God, Thou who
art worthy of eternal praise and fame, and blessed
be Thy revered and glorious name in all eternity.
May Thy angels glorify Thee, and all the saints
proclaim Thy praise. For Thou art great in Thy
might, and Thy wisdom is unfathomable, and Thy
mercy is greater than all Thy works. I will
glorify Thee, O Lord, as long as I live, and sing of
Thy holy name as long as I exist. For Thou hast
cheered me with Thy mercy and filled my mouth
with rejoicings. Thou hast snatched me from
violent torrents, and saved me from deep whirl-
pools, and placed my feet on safe ground. I was
distant from Thee, O God, and eternal sweetness,
but Thou hast had mercy upon me, and hast come
here unto me. I erred, but Thou didst admonish
me. I wandered about, knowing not whither to
go, but Thou didst lead me on the right path. I had
gone astray from Thee and lost both Thee and my-

self, but appearing to me, Thou broughtest me back to myself. I had gone as far as the bitterness of hell, but Thou, tearing me back, hast led me to the sweetness of heaven. Therefore may my soul bless its Lord, and my whole innermost mind praise His holy name. My heart is ready, my heart is ready; I will sing and rejoice in Thee. For Thou art higher than all height and deeper than all depth, wonderful, glorious, and full of mercy. Woe to the foolish souls who leave Thee and think that they will find solace elsewhere, for it exists but in Thee. Neither the earth nor the abyss have it. There in Thee alone is there eternal rest. Heaven and earth are Thy works, and they are good and beautiful and desirable, because they are Thy works. Yet are they not as good, as beautiful, as desirable as Thou, their Creator. Therefore can they not entirely fill up and satiate the spirits that seek solace. Thou art, O Lord, the plenitude of plenitudes! Late became I enamoured of Thee, O Eternal Beauty, for late did I know Thee. But I know Thee when Thou gleamest on me, O Heavenly Light! Let him refrain from Thy praise who knows not Thy mercy. But may my innermost mind profess the Lord. Oh, who will grant it to me, that my heart be intoxicated by Thee, O Eternal Odour, that I may forget everything that is not Thee, O my God? Conceal Thyself no longer from my heart, O most beauteous of beauties! If worldly things obscure Thee to me, I die. May I but behold Thee, be with Thee, never lose Thee again! Uphold me, O Lord, guide me, support me, that I may not stray from Thee and slip! Grant that I may love Thee with an eternal love, and that I may love besides Thee no other things, except for Thy sake, and in Thee, O Infinitive Love! But what more should I say, O my Lord? I am here; I am Thine. I am Thine own; I am Thine for ever. I renounce heaven and earth that I may have Thee. Do not withdraw Thyself from me. I have enough that is unchangeable through all eternity; I have enough in Thee alone. My soul and my body rejoice in Thee, the living God. When, then, shall I come to Thee, and appear before Thy countenance? When Thou wishest, O my Lord God, take me! I am here; I am ready. Call me when Thou wilt, where Thou wilt, how Thou wilt, I will go whither Thou orderest; I will do that which Thou dost command. May but Thy good spirit direct me and lead me through the snares of the world as through an even country, and may Thy mercy guide me on my way, and lead me through the—alas!—doleful darkness of the world to eternal light!

" Amen and Amen."

" Gloria in excelsis Deo et in terra Pax Hominibus bonæ Voluntatis."

THE END

Printed by Cowan & Co., Ltd., Perth.

CPSIA information can be obtained
at www.ICGtesting.com
Printed in the USA
LVOW13s2309310117
522812LV00016B/277/P